# LET MY PEOPLE VOTE

# LET MY PEOPLE VOTE

## MY BATTLE TO RESTORE THE CIVIL
## RIGHTS OF RETURNING CITIZENS

DESMOND MEADE

BEACON PRESS
BOSTON

Beacon Press
Boston, Massachusetts
www.beacon.org

Beacon Press books
are published under the auspices of
the Unitarian Universalist Association of Congregations.

23 22 21 20     8 7 6 5 4 3 2 1

This book is printed on acid-free paper that meets the uncoated paper
ANSI/NISO specifications for permanence as revised in 1992.

Text design and composition by Kim Arney

*Library of Congress Cataloging-in-Publication Data*

Names: Meade, Desmond, author.
Title: Let my people vote : my battle to restore the civil rights of returning
    citizens / Desmond Meade.
Description: Boston : Beacon Press, 2020.
Identifiers: LCCN 2020022049 (print) | LCCN 2020022050 (ebook) |
    ISBN 9780807062326 (hardcover) | ISBN 9780807062555 (ebook)
Subjects: LCSH: Meade, Desmond, 1967- | Ex-convicts—Civil rights—Florida. |
    Ex-convicts—Legal status, laws, etc.—Florida. | Political rights,
    Loss of—United States—States. | Ex-convicts—Suffrage—Florida. |
    Post-conviction remedies—Florida. | Ex-convicts—Florida—Biography. |
    Lawyers—Florida—Biography. | African American lawyers—Florida—Biography.
Classification: LCC KFF565.F6 M43 2020 (print) | LCC KFF565.F6 (ebook) |
    DDC 342.759/072086927—dc23
LC record available at https://lccn.loc.gov/2020022049
LC ebook record available at https://lccn.loc.gov/2020022050

# CONTENTS

# LET MY PEOPLE VOTE

# LOVE HAS WON THE DAY

ON JANUARY 8, 2018, I registered to vote. I was fifty years old. It wasn't a lack of civic interest that had kept me away from the polls before. Rather I, like approximately 1.4 million Floridians, had been denied the right to vote, along with other civil rights, such as the right to serve on a jury or to hold public office, because of our felony convictions. The citizens' initiative for an amendment to the state constitution that my organization, the Florida Rights Restoration Coalition, had spearheaded changed all that.

You would think that the new governor of the state of Florida being sworn in would be the biggest news story, as his inauguration happened on the same day. But the headline was people like me embracing our role in the democratic process. If you were to believe the papers, you would have expected ex-felons—whom we called returning citizens—would have been turned away. Some thought the supervisors of elections across the state of Florida were going to have barricades erected or use fire hoses, and that there would be police who said, "Oh no, you can't register yet, not until the governor says so." Some supporters of our ballot initiative were even organizing protests against offices they were sure would deny people the ability to register to vote. That is the legacy of trauma in this country that has been hard to overcome, the omnipresence of prejudice and discrimination that shapes what we have come to expect and fear in this country, even in the twenty-first century.

But the exact opposite happened on January 8. Voter registration agencies rolled out the red carpet. Some had balloons and confetti. You might have seen a shot of me covered in confetti that they popped from a pressurized bottle as I came out of the agency with my voter registration card in hand. You might have also seen some tears. There were so many tears of joy throughout the state of Florida. I took my family with me to go register because it was their votes on my behalf that had contributed to our successful proposed amendment, known as Amendment 4. My wife and my two sons voted yes for me because they loved me.

My daughter was actually the one to register me to vote, right in the elections office. I had one of my younger sons register for the first time along with me. I had been registered before, as a young man, but there was a guy there who had lost the right to vote before he was even eighteen. When Amendment 4 passed, not only did he register to vote for the first time, but he also brought his son, who was eighteen, along with him so they could register together. You had some people who registered to vote that day who had last voted for John F. Kennedy. You had people register to vote who were in their sixties and had never voted before in their lives.

Folks brought their family and their friends and their loved ones. Even supervisors in the election offices were crying. We were celebrating the expansion of democracy. We were celebrating the fact that what got us here was love. Just the previous November, our ballot initiative had passed by a margin of more than three hundred thousand people. We won based on inclusion and bringing people together. We showed the world that love can move major policy issues and get support from Democrats, Republicans, independents, who were white, Black, and Latino, rich and poor. I remember telling everyone with ears, "Love has won the day."

That love extended to those who were now able to come out of the shadows about their own felony convictions. When I was out on the campaign trail collecting petitions, I would run across people who had been married for ten or fifteen years, and their spouse never knew their partner had a felony conviction. They had hidden that part of their lives from their loved ones, and I understood that as a returning citizen myself. There's a pain that we have for the things that we did, for the pain that we created in the lives of our family and our friends, and in some cases, the people we've caused harm to. Amendment 4 gave a lot of people the courage to take an affirmative step to make amends in a positive way by registering to vote.

You may think the right to vote is a small matter, and if you do, I would bet you have never had it taken away from you. My wife, Sheena, ran for the Florida State House in 2016, and I couldn't even vote for her. Things like that are the difference between contribution to a cause and commitment to one. Both are good things, and both are needed, but there are folks who believe in something just enough to contribute to it, and there are those who believe in something so much that they are willing to make a sacrifice. I, like so many others, was forced to live in a reality that I would never be able to vote again as long as I lived in Florida. I have heard people say they hoped they could vote before they die because they wanted to know what it was like to feel like a citizen again, and I could understand that.

Voting can, of course, help you elect people who are paying greater attention to the particular needs of your communities, so it is practical. But it's also a symbol. Out of all the rights stripped from men and women returning to society after serving time in prison, voting is really the only one that says *I am a citizen of this country, and my voice does matter.* You don't have to vote if you don't want to, but having the right to vote, that is what solidifies you as a person of consequence more than anything else in the world. That is especially important for people like me who made mistakes or suffered through addiction. We were made to feel we weren't part of society anymore, that we were the lowest of the low. We were despised because of our addiction. We were despised because of the crimes we may have committed. What the right to vote says is that I'm somebody again. It says, simply and powerfully, I AM.

The right to vote is one of many rights that need to be restored to individuals who have a previous felony conviction. According to Florida statutes, anyone who's convicted of any felony offense—and here we could be talking about driving with a suspended license or even tampering with an odometer—automatically loses their right to serve on a jury, to run for office, to own a firearm, and to vote. Those are the four basic civil rights that a person would lose, but other restrictions are even more immediately problematic. The collateral consequences of having a felony record, such as occupational license restrictions and the effective narrowing of job opportunities and options (you have to check that box on your job applications in most localities, and that means that many, if not most, jobs are off-limits for you), housing restrictions (you can't live in most publicly funded housing, and many homeowner associations have restrictions in their bylaws against owning or even renting a home in certain areas until your rights have been restored), and education restrictions (such as the inability to receive government-backed school loans if you have been convicted of certain crimes).

These collateral consequences are far-reaching and profound, and so are the effects of not having your rights restored. Without being able to get good, safe, and stable housing and decent job and educational opportunities, returning citizens cannot reintegrate back into their community, and their story is going to be written completely differently. Chances are much better that a returning citizen is going to recidivate, meaning relapsing or regressing into crime. In a study done by the Florida Parole Commission in 2011, only 11.1 percent of individuals who had their civil rights restored during the calendar years of 2009 and 2010 reoffended and were forced to return to incarceration or community supervision. The overall recidivism rate for inmates released from 2001 to 2008, on the other hand, was 33.1 percent.

That is a factor of three, and the numbers don't change much if you take a different slice of the statistical pie. According to the Washington Economics Group (WEG), the average three-year recidivism rate for felons released in 2012 under the clemency system in place then was 25.2 percent. However, the three-year recidivism rate for felons released in 2009 who had their voting and other civil rights restored under the previous clemency system was only 12.4 percent. Why it matters that between 51 percent and 66 percent of previously convicted felons don't return to crime is likely pretty obvious, beginning with the fact that the reduction of recidivism is essential to curtail crime and increase public safety.

Then you consider the economic impact. According to State of Florida sources, it costs taxpayers over twenty thousand dollars per year to incarcerate each prison inmate. If you just consider the 27,266 individuals whose rights were restored in 2009 and 2010 who did not recidivate, that's a savings of half a billion dollars alone, money that could be reallocated to places of need such as education.

There are other economic benefits to seeing the recidivism rate go down. Administrative and court costs to taxpayers decline, while the increased employment and earnings of eligible individuals convicted of a felony broadens the tax base, relieving some of the burdens placed on existing citizens. WEG calculated that, over time, the combined economic impact of restoring rights to returning citizens would support close to 3,800 new jobs annually, with an increase in annual household income for Florida residents of $151 million. That's a total annual economic impact of $365 million.

These numbers are not theoretical, nor are they wishful thinking. The connection of a decrease in recidivism with an increase in opportunities and respect is something I know from my own heart too. When I was in prison, I didn't daydream, *Man, I cannot wait to get out so I can commit more crime and hurt more people and have myself locked up all over again.* What I envisioned, as did most of the folks that I knew who were incarcerated, was, *Man, when I get out, I want my life to improve. I don't want to come back to prison. I want to be loved. I want to have a family. I want to be able to have nice things and maybe I can make amends to folks I hurt, and I need to find a way to do it.*

The right to vote is the first right my organization, the Florida Rights Restoration Coalition, went after, because we knew how powerful it would be if the very same people who were told they don't deserve to have their voices heard could come together. Inevitably that kind of voting bloc would be able to draw attention to whatever issues it felt most strongly about. Being able to vote may not be the key to getting your life back together, but with the passage of Amendment 4—the largest expansion of American democracy in fifty years—it is an excellent start. In every county of Florida, people from all walks of life and political backgrounds registered to vote, putting elected officials on notice that their responsiveness was now being watched and evaluated with an eye to action and consequence.

Finally, there is a moral imperative to treat others with dignity, to never let the punishment—or the lingering effects of a punishment that is, in effect, a continued punishment—exceed the crime. I have known people who have made mistakes or committed a crime many, many years before and died without ever knowing that their rights had been restored. In the election of 2012, the Florida State Board of Executive Clemency, which administered the restoration of civil rights, revealed that about 14,000 people may not have known that their civil rights had been restored. Many of them didn't know because they had moved and never received their notification in the mail. As a result, all of those voter certifications were returned to the clemency board. I was living in Miami at the time, and I took it upon myself to try to locate as many people in my area as possible, to let them know their rights had been restored and that they should go register to vote and participate in the election.

I remember it was a Saturday morning, and it was one of those somber-looking days. The sky looked like it would just burst open any moment. There was one particular person that I had spent a couple days looking for. When I finally found his house, it started to rain. Just as I was about to knock on his door, a neighbor told me he had died a month before. This man's criminal history had some charges like possession of cocaine. But after a certain year, there were no more arrests. Maybe he had gone to treatment, as I had. Maybe he'd recovered from his addiction. Whatever the case, he never got in trouble again, so it was clear he had turned his life around.

I remember watching the rain coming down in sheets now outside my car window, tears streaming down from my eyes. This guy had died and didn't even know he had accomplished this great thing. When we get into recovery, those milestones mean something. It's almost like a vindication: Okay, yeah, you messed up. But now you're doing good.

Getting your civil rights back is not something that's easily done in the state of Florida. This is my story about how we were able to do it, and not just for 14,000 people but for an estimated 1.4 million people.

# ONE

# THE RAILROAD TRACKS

I HAD BEEN IN AND OUT of three drug treatment programs by the time August 2005 rolled around. I was thirty-eight years old then and still struggling to get my life together. My mother had passed away, and I had caused so much hurt to my family that they could no longer be a resource to me. I was not the same person that they were accustomed to seeing; my addiction to crack cocaine had caused me to behave erratically. The previous two treatment programs I had enrolled in were reputable, and it was me who couldn't stay the course. The one I was in that August was a sham.

I've been in the recovery business for a while. I've helped manage three quarter-way houses, so I've seen the whole process: all of the tricks, all of the different challenges, all of the fights that people are going through within themselves.

I know a lot of times we addicts will put the blame on other people and circumstances beyond our control. But I'm telling you, as a sober person looking back on the program I was in at that time, it was a sham. They were more concerned with what they could get out of you, like your food stamps, than with helping you. You had to turn over your food stamps to them, and if you didn't have food stamps, they wanted to make you apply for food stamps. It wasn't even necessarily recovery focused. But either way, I was there, and I was trying to stick it out.

Then I injured my back. The people in charge of the treatment center told me that I could not go to the doctor. If I left the premises,

I would get kicked out of the program. To this day, I have no clue why that was. Would they lose funding if someone were off their rolls for a few days? Did they think I was faking my injury so I could get some pain medication and use that as a gateway back to using more heavily? I actually got kind of pissed off. Why would someone deny me the opportunity to get medical help when my back was really hurting?

I chose to go see the doctor, and the program told me I couldn't come back. So I went to a homeless shelter where I had been housed before.

One of the counselors recognized me and said, "Wait a minute. Didn't we send you to a program?"

I said, "Yeah, but I had to leave, and they kicked me out."

And the counselor told me, "Well, you can't stay here."

And so I got kicked out of that shelter as well. I was back out on the streets. I found a different shelter where I was able to stay for one night. At this particular place, you have to be back by a certain time or you lose your bed. I went to visit my sister, and I came back about five minutes late and I had lost my spot. Now, I was really out of luck. I found a spot behind a dumpster and I crashed for the night.


THE NEXT DAY, I CALLED A FRIEND OF MINE ON THE PHONE. HE WAS A GOOD FRIEND, AN old friend.

I said, "Man, I need some money."

He told me, "I don't have money. But I think I might have something a little bit better than that. I know this pastor of a church. If you let her pray for you, your life is gonna turn around."

I remember when he told me that, something came over me, so I developed a great yearning to do exactly that. I wanted to meet this pastor. I wanted to have this pastor pray for me because I was just frustrated and tired of the life that I was living. I was so tired of using drugs. I was desperate. I was ready for anything.

The church was quite a distance from where I was standing at that moment. I looked through my pockets, to find the last bits of change I had to my name. I figured that if I was going to spend this money, I was going to step out on faith, because this person was going to pray for me and my life was going to change. It was gonna be worth it. I believed that something special was going to happen that day.

As it turned out, I didn't have enough money to both take a bus and get the transfer to another line that I needed to take. I only had enough to just take one straight shot, so I walked to one location to catch a particular bus that would drop me off not too far from this church. I walked a mile from the bus stop, following the directions carefully.

When I got there that night, they were having a service. I thought that was a good sign. In fact, they were just beginning when I walked in. I went to sit all the way in the back, because I wasn't the best dressed. But I enjoyed the service: the music, the singing—it kind of brought me back to my younger days; I'd been raised in the church where my father was the pastor.

By the end of the service, I had been uplifted by a combination of the preaching and my childhood memories. I felt inspired with a certain confidence, so I walked to the front of the church and approached the pastor. I told her I was homeless and desperate, but I wanted to qualify that for her.

I remember telling her, "Pastor, I'm not looking for money. I'm not looking for clothes. I'm not looking for anything but prayer. A friend of mine told me to come to you and ask you to pray for me because my life has just been out of control."

She put her hands on my shoulder in such a loving way. I thought for sure she was getting ready to pop out the olive oil and anoint my forehead with one of those life transformational prayers. Instead, she pointed to another guy that was in the church.

"You see that gentleman over there?"

"Yes, ma'am."

"Go talk to him and have him set up an appointment for you for tomorrow."

In my mind, I thought: *Woman, don't you understand what I'm telling you? Don't you understand my level of desperation? Tomorrow? Do you understand the space that I'm in right now? That I just spent my last cent to come here and all I wanted was a prayer, and you're telling me to come back tomorrow? How the hell am I going to get home? Where am I going to stay tonight?*

I didn't say any of this. I just told her yes, but I walked right past the guy and out of the church. When I stepped out into the humid, night air, the thought that stayed with me was,

Man, even God has abandoned me. Even God has turned His back on me.

THAT WAS A VERY LOW POINT IN MY LIFE, THINKING THAT NO ONE LOVED ME. EVEN GOD, the all-forgiving God, didn't want to have anything to do with me. I didn't know what to do when I walked out of that church, so I walked the mile back to the bus line from where I had come.

And as I got near the stop, I remembered that my mother had a good friend who owned a restaurant nearby. My mom was a waitress back in the day, and there were these two cooks who were real close with her over a period of about fifteen years. During that time, one of the cooks ended up leaving and starting his own restaurant, and that restaurant was not too far from here. So I kept walking, thinking, *Maybe I can go to him, because I'm stuck, and see if I can get a few dollars based off his friendship with our family, in particular with my mom.*

Thankfully, he was there. He gave me twenty dollars. Typically, I get twenty dollars, the first place I'm going is to the drug hole, right? But I was tired. I really didn't want to use drugs. And I didn't buy any alcohol. I used that money to get some snacks to eat, and a grape soda, and to catch a bus back toward downtown Miami. I got off near the major hospitals and the Miami-Dade County jail. It was now the middle of the night. And that night, for the first time in my entire life, I slept on a bus bench.

I was tired. Before, maybe even the day before, I would not have thought about sleeping out in the open. I would have slept inside an abandoned building, or if it had to be outside, it would have been in a park or behind a church, someplace where people wouldn't see me. But that night, all my pride was gone. I just wanted to lay down, and I didn't care where. I went to sleep in full view of the public.

THE NEXT MORNING WHEN I WOKE UP, I THOUGHT, *OKAY, I'M GOING TO GET SOME HELP.* I tried to get into one more drug treatment program. They did a urinalysis, and I still had cocaine in my system so they couldn't accept me.

The funny thing about some of these programs is that to get in, you have to be clean, which didn't make any sense to me. I was there to get help because I have a drug problem, but I can't have drugs in my system to be there.

That's when I thought about Central Intake. Central Intake is a facility that's part of the Jackson Memorial Hospital program, almost like a clearinghouse for drug and alcohol treatment centers. It deals with abuse at a crisis level. It's a place where you can go to be evaluated, and then, based on the assessment, they recommend you for different types of programs, whether inpatient or outpatient.

Central Intake was another two miles away. I was walking in this thick humidity under a hot sun and I was frustrated as hell. I had never eaten out of a dumpster before that day, but I had no more pride. Another homeless guy told me where there was some Popeye's chicken, and it didn't matter to me anymore that I was diving into the trash to get some for myself. Before—sure, I would have had my standards. But with the sweat rolling down my back, thinking about last night where God forgot all about me, feeling dejected as I headed toward Central Intake, I just didn't care anymore.

And that's how I ended up at the railroad tracks. I had to cross these railroad tracks to get to Central Intake. It was a desolate place. You could tell the area was used a lot by homeless people, with garbage strewn all over the place. People discard their refuse there and that's exactly how I felt, like I was useless, worthless. I stood there, a broken man. I was homeless. I was addicted to drugs. I had only recently been released from prison, so of course I was unemployed. I didn't have anything; I didn't own anything other than the clothes that were on my back. I knew that my loving mother didn't raise me to be in that position, but there I was. I didn't see any light at the end of the tunnel, and I was ready to check out. I was ready to end it all.

As I stood there fixated, I was able to block out the oppressive heat and humidity and become oblivious to everything else. I didn't hear the traffic passing by on the nearby boulevards. I didn't see anyone in and around their houses or apartment buildings. I had a laser focus on the railroad tracks.

My mind went back to a story I had read a few weeks prior about a man in Broward County who had committed suicide by jumping in front of a train. I was so riveted by that story, I couldn't take another step. *How did he do it?* I wondered. *Did he wait until the train was too close to stop in time, and then jumped in front of it at the last second? What did he experience? Did the train kill him instantly? Did it cut him in half? Was it the weight of the train that severed him, or was his body crushed between the steel wheels and the iron tracks?*

The only thing that was going through my mind as I stood there was how much pain I was going to feel when I jumped in front of the oncoming train. I was thinking about whether I was going to die instantly, or if I'd have to go through moments of agonizing pain.

I was staring at the curve where the train was going to come around the bend. And I could not leave. I could not cross those tracks. That was the end of the road for me. I was just waiting. And I waited.

I have no idea how long I waited, because I was so empty. I'm sure someone had identified me already out there; maybe there were people whispering at that very moment, "There's a crazy man out there!" But I was oblivious to their concerns, and I wouldn't have responded to them anyway. Or maybe I was invisible to them, just like homeless people are to so many of us. Either way I wouldn't have cared about who saw me or what they were thinking because I was ready to end my life. But for some reason that train didn't come that day. I waited there for what felt like hours because of the zone I was in, and the train just didn't come.

Eventually I was able to break my chain of thought and cross the tracks. Central Intake was only two blocks away. *Let's give it that last shot*, I thought. I crossed the tracks and walked the two blocks, and they got me into an inpatient program. It's one thing for them to evaluate you, that's just one hurdle. Then they have to find space in a program. It just so happened that I was there at the right time, and the program had space, the type of program that they thought I needed.

That same day, they transported me to the site of the program, which I completed over the course of the next four months. I was grateful that I had been given another opportunity to beat my drug addiction, but I was also concerned about whether or not my life would ever amount to anything.

# TWO

# SEARCHING FOR PURPOSE

A S SOON AS I CROSSED THE TRACKS, I stopped and asked myself a question that I believe helped change the course of my life.

I had asked myself, "Desmond, if you were to have died, if that train were to have run you over and killed you, how many people would come to your funeral?"

Now, the immediate answer was zero. Because I was homeless, my family didn't know where I was. I wasn't trying to hang out with any of my friends because of the shame of being a drug addict. The area where I was, it was not in my usual neighborhood. I didn't even have proper ID on me. Would I have been buried in a pauper's grave? I didn't know how that kind of thing worked, if I would be identified by my dental records or something like that.

*Let's say they did identify me* . . . I continued the internal discussion with myself. Let's say in this scenario, I was killed by the train, but the local paper, the *Miami Herald*, got wind of it. Let's say they put my picture on the front page with the headline in big, bold letters, "Desmond Meade Killed by Train." Now how many people would come to my funeral? And after thinking long and hard I only came up with four people: my two sisters, Lucinda and Annette, and my two nieces, Kathleen and Elizabeth. And out of those four people, only my nieces would have shed a tear because they were still at an age where they believed in me. I could just hear the narrative, you know? *Man, he had so much promise if it wasn't for those drugs.*

Only being able to come up with four people, that thought hit me in the gut like a Mike Tyson blow. It really took the wind out of me. I had a powerful moment of realization, as I stood there looking back at the tracks. It made me question myself: *Desmond, you mean to tell me after all these years of living on this planet, after all the relationships and friendships and your time in the military and the places that you've lived and visited, after all your travel, that only four people would care if you died? Has your life been that insignificant?*

What have I been doing with the time that I have spent on this planet so far? What has it come to? Was my life going to end with a whimper and not a bang? I didn't like that one bit.

I REMEMBER TAKING THAT FEELING WITH ME WHEN I WALKED THOSE TWO BLOCKS TO Central Intake, because it was the exact opposite of how I had viewed or imagined funerals to be. I was born in Saint Croix, US Virgin Islands, in a little subdivision of the city of Christiansted, called Peters Rest. One of my earliest memories, something that really stuck with me, was a big funeral of someone famous who had died on the island. I remember going to church and it seemed like there were hundreds and hundreds of people who came to the service. It was a sad moment for a lot of people. I can still see the tears in their eyes. But it was also wondrous to me: Who could this person have been to have that much of an impact on so many other people?

I was always somebody who wanted to be loved like that. I think we all have an internal compass to get to a space where you feel love and comfort and safety. Some folks may ignore it; some may acknowledge and embrace it.

I was the type of kid that my mom did not have to ask to do something twice. I was her baby, and I had an undying love for her. Her birthstone was a ruby, and any time I saw some trinket at the Cuban bodega that featured ruby-like jewels, I would buy it for her.

When we first moved to Miami from Saint Croix, it was just me, my mom, and my dad. Then, one by one, my brothers and sisters came over to the United States. Pretty soon, we had six of us under one roof. Growing up, I always looked at everybody in the household as one family. I didn't know the difference between stepbrothers and stepsisters. I didn't realize at the time that my mom and dad were not married.

Looking back now, I knew that I was excited about the idea of family. The desire to love and be loved was something that was just inherent in me. I picked up that some of my siblings were probably not reciprocating that love like I thought they should, and I always used to struggle with that, not realizing that we weren't that so-called complete family like I thought we were.

Throughout a major portion of my young and young adult life I was confused and never really got the full story. It wasn't until the death of my father that the story came out. Basically, my dad left his family to be with my mom. The tales that I heard indicated that I was an illegitimate child, and that I was the apple of his eye. Looking back now, I could see the sibling rivalry that was going on. It actually answered a lot of questions. I was flooded with memories of one brother telling me that I wasn't really his brother; on a separate occasion, he told me that I stole his dad. Another time at school I overheard one of my other siblings tell someone that I was their cousin. *I can't be a cousin and a brother at the same time*, I thought. Those things played a role in my developing psyche and fueled my yearning to be accepted, particularly by my family, that has stayed with me up until today.

Being from a different family tree, so to speak, left me with an internalized pain that I suppressed. Even though I didn't acknowledge it consciously, there was still a need to numb it. And so, that love I was seeking, that comfort, became connected with alcohol pretty early on in my life. We used to have these parties . . . maybe it would be somebody's birthday party. The church folks would be there, and then after the church folks left, they'd bring the liquor out and the rum corks would start popping. I remember that these were some of the best times I had, when everybody was festive and there was a lot of love flowing around. I associated drinking with happiness and that set the stage later for drugs to become my comforter.

A LOT OF THESE THINGS CAME OUT IN THE TREATMENT PROGRAM WHERE I WAS SENT BY Central Intake. They asked us to do things like write in a journal, compose letters to our siblings, and talk about our past. One by one, memories would come back to me that had been locked in my subconscious.

I thought about it this way: sometimes I have trouble thinking of the name of a kid I went to elementary school with. I could try my hardest and still not remember it. But a few days later I might be riding in my car, and a song comes on the radio from back then, and his name will just pop right back up into my conscious mind.

Certain things can trigger our memory or break things out of our subconscious, but a good treatment program doesn't leave those things to chance, like a random song coming over the airwaves. They ask us to apply ourselves because what we've suppressed is exactly what is playing a key role in our abuse of drugs or alcohol.

So that was my frame of mind after a month or two of being in drug treatment. I guess you could say that the door between my subconscious and my conscious mind was swinging pretty freely by that point. I remember I was by myself in the room in the drug treatment facility that held the television. Rosa Parks had just passed away, and thousands of people were coming to Washington, DC, to pay their last respects. Tears were streaming down everyone's cheeks as her body lay in state in the Capitol Rotunda. I was captivated by the outpouring of emotions, how she had touched everyone so personally.

As I looked up at the television, which was mounted high on the wall, my mind went back to a funeral I had witnessed as a young boy in Saint Croix. I instantly became overwhelmed. It was like I got a bolt of energy, and I jumped out of my chair. I started screaming and pointing at the TV, saying, "That's it! That's it! That's what I want! When I die, I want thousands of people to mourn me. I want people to feel sorrow when I die."

I knew right there and then that I wanted the big funeral. I wanted people to mourn me, lots of people. My mind raced as I started to try to plan my funeral. I was scrambling in my head to figure out how I was going to get that kind of funeral to happen for me. What am I going to have to do to make people feel sad that I passed away? I didn't want to be that person who died and nobody came to the funeral or even knew that he died.

———————

THE FIRST THING MY RACING MIND DECIDED ON WAS THE LOCATION FOR THE FUNERAL. I needed a venue that was big enough to hold a large capacity of people. I quickly landed on a stadium. It would be the same stadium where the Miami Dolphins football team plays. It's called Hard Rock Stadium now, but back then it was called Joe Robbie Stadium, after the Miami Dolphins' founder. I wanted that whole entire stadium to be filled. And then I also wanted seats on the field, as well as people standing—standing room only; the arena would be just full of people who were sad because I died. There wasn't going to be a dry eye in the entire stadium. That felt good. I got the venue.

Then I got stuck with the next question. *What type of person can command that type of audience?* In order for me to have the funeral that I wanted, I had to somehow or other impact somebody's life, a whole bunch of people's lives. Joe Robbie Stadium held a lot of people, so that was a lot of lives I had to impact. I didn't know how I was going to do it, but I just knew that that's what I needed to do. That was the only thing I could hold on to at that moment.

I knew I'd have to be some kind of celebrity, and I landed on either being an athlete or an actor.

The thing is, I didn't think I could be an athlete because I have bad knees from playing football in junior high and high school. So the only thing left was for me to become a movie star. The actor who came to mind, when I started thinking about stars, was Denzel Washington. Right? Everybody just loves Denzel Washington. The ladies are crazy for him; he can't do any wrong.

Now, at the time I didn't think I was a bad-looking guy, but I didn't think I was the Denzel Washington type of handsome. I sometimes look back on that day and thank God I didn't think of Forest Whitaker, because then I think I might have felt I had a shot. You know, if he can make it, I can make it too. But I didn't think of Forest Whitaker that day or anyone else other than Denzel Washington. And I knew I wasn't him.

Out of options, I became disappointed because I couldn't determine what I could do to command the type of audience I wanted. But that disappointment did not last for long because my thoughts returned to Rosa Parks. I remembered listening to interviews with her and some feature stories about her. I started thinking about how she did one thing that people remembered. She refused to give up her seat on the bus. That one act she committed (or refused to commit) endeared her to a lot of folks, although the truth is she was an activist her entire life and had done thousands of things for civil rights both before and after that day in Montgomery.

I thought, *Well, maybe if I can take all of the pain, and suffering, and low self-esteem, all that stuff that came together and led me to the railroad tracks and had me thinking about killing myself, if I could take those very same things, maybe I could package it in a positive way to help other people so they don't have to end up at those railroad tracks, that could be a start.*

If I could help change someone's life, then they could, in turn, change other lives. It would be like that old commercial about "you tell two friends and they tell two friends" and so on, and so on. Pretty soon, there would be a lot of people who when I die would be able to say, "Man, if it wasn't for Desmond helping that person, and that person helping whomever, my life would not have been as good as it is today."

And so I figured that my best shot was just to help someone else. I didn't have a clue where to start, or what to do to make that happen, but I knew that I had to make a difference in other people's lives. I had to take my small personal tragedy and use it to help someone else triumph in life.

# THREE

# DOWN ON MY KNEES

L ET ME BACK UP. The year before my lowest point led me to the railroad
tracks, I was released from prison. I had served three years of a
fifteen-year term for illegal possession of a firearm by a known felon.
That was November of 2004, when I was released from the South
Florida Reception Center in Miami-Dade County, the same county
where my final appeal was heard, and the fifteen-year sentence I originally received was officially reversed and remanded to the time I had
served so far.

Typically, when someone is released from prison, they are given
a check or a money order for something like a hundred dollars, and
they put you on a bus or a train to the city or station that's closest to
your last known address. In my case, I was taken to the metro rail
station and put on a train to downtown Miami. The thing about this
is, though, when they release people, it's typically in the dead of the
night. You're putting people who have been on the inside for years
back on the streets in the middle of the night.

I don't know why they would do that. It's a contrapositive. There's
nothing open but the bars and the drug holes. If you're releasing
someone who has struggles with addiction, what's he going to do?
Even if I wanted to do the right thing, there's no one on the street but
drug dealers. There's no program you can go to because everything is
closed. You're just left to fend for yourself.

I had made up my mind that I wasn't going to use drugs and instead was going to try to get into a homeless shelter as quickly as

possible. I thought a beer wouldn't hurt though, so I found an open restaurant and went in and ordered some chicken wings and a Presidente. I remembered that brand because the whole time I was incarcerated I would watch beer commercials during football season. They really knew how to make a beer look cold and refreshing.

I couldn't even drink the whole bottle. I thought it was the nastiest-tasting thing I ever tasted, and maybe that meant I was on the right road. I hadn't had a drink or used drugs in prison; it was like that overwhelming urge went dormant, even though it was easy to get on the inside. Some folks think it's easier to get drugs in prison than when you're out. But the minute I got out and life hit, my struggles resumed.

I went back into the streets and was able to flag down a police officer.

I told him, "Listen. I'm just released from prison. I don't want to go back. I don't want to get in trouble. Could you help me get into a homeless shelter?"

And miraculously, he did. He took me to a place called The Hack, which is the nickname for Chapman Partnership. And that's where I spent my first night after being released from prison.

The Community Partnership for the Prevention of Homelessness, now known as Chapman Partnership, didn't look like a typical homeless shelter. It's a really pretty building. I used to think that it was a technical building when I walked past it. In my mind, when I think of a homeless shelter, it usually is as it is depicted in the movies: a dark and dirty place where despondent people are hanging around the block. It's a dangerous place to be.

Chapman Partnership was different, inside and out. The staff and the administration were really great people. They didn't necessarily look down on you, and they had a sincere desire to help you overcome homelessness. They wanted to help you get yourself together. One thing I didn't tell them when I went in was that I had a drug problem; I figured I didn't have a drug problem anymore because when I was in prison I hadn't used drugs. I think most people, when they get out, would be looking to get a place to live and a job. Those are the top two priorities. So that's all I wanted from them, help with those two things. They were able to help me within thirty days, first to get some proper identification. Then they helped me get a job and find a place of my own to live.

I messed that up real quick, though, because as soon as I got a job and started getting my checks—as soon as I really had freedom—I went right back to using drugs. I would lose everything and then I would be right back at Chapman Partnership again, trying to start over. That's the cycle that I remained in from the time I was released until the time I was in front of those railroad tracks in August of 2005. It was always have a job, get a check, end up using, maybe lose the job or not go to work, and have to just keep doing it over and over and over again.

I'd had more than one chance, right? I'd had multiple chances. But one thing I've learned is that when you're battling addiction, sometimes you're going to need multiple chances. Not too many people get it on the first go-round. It just took some time for me to get it, a whole lot of time in my case.

ONCE I COMPLETED MY FOUR-MONTH DRUG TREATMENT PROGRAM AFTER MY DAY AT THE railroad tracks, I came back to Chapman Partnership to live. When someone completes treatment they're either going to a three-quarter-way house (more on that soon), or maybe they're going back to their family, if they haven't burned that bridge. I probably could've gone back to family, but I didn't choose that route.

I always had the mindset that if I did something wrong, I would at least try to minimize the amount of suffering that my family would have to go through.

When I was arrested, I could have asked them for bail money or to post a bond for me. But I believe that everything that I've gotten into, I've had some role to play in it. I don't think that there's a case where I was just completely innocent. If I had to do time for doing something wrong, that should only be my burden. I never wanted to saddle my family with it. I had never been a person who called home every day. I would call every once in a while, just to let them know that I was okay. Maybe I would write a letter here and there. But I never asked for money for the commissary, for example. I didn't think that my family should have to pay for whatever I'd done wrong or the situation I had put myself in. Of course, there is some shame involved, too, in not wanting them to see too clearly how far their Desmond had fallen. And there was another part that said that if they were not included in the spoils of my doings, then I should not include them in the misery either.

Another reason why I didn't feel the need to go back home was that I had begun to discover my purpose. Throughout my entire life, I've always tried to fit in somewhere, to find my niche. As I've told you, I always wanted to be loved by my family. That grew into wanting to be a part of a team, a school, a community. I had such a yearning to find the place in life where I belonged. I was searching for something and I didn't even know what it was. We all go through life wondering, *Why am I here? What is it that I'm supposed to do? Isn't there some special reason I was born? If not, why was I created?*

At the end of my four-month drug treatment, I went to one final group therapy session. They brought in some folks who weren't as far along as we were to hear our stories and what we had come to understand. I spoke about a number of the issues that related to my addiction. I don't remember exactly what I said because, as would be true later when I led a convening or had the occasion to speak publicly to large groups, I never brought any notes with me. I always simply spoke from the heart.

After the session, we all stepped outside. And that was when a young man approached me. He told me that something I said had caused him to experience a significant shift in his thinking. Through my being so open, he felt like he had a much brighter outlook on life, and he just wanted to thank me. He now believed that when the time came for him to leave the program, he could live a better life.

I so wish I could remember the exact words he said to me. I can picture him: a young guy, with a scruffy little beard. I could help an artist draw a picture of where we were standing, the building we had just come out of, how we were four steps away from the building and he was smoking a cigarette. I may not be able to remember the specific words he spoke, but I can hear to this day how much hope there was in his voice, as clear as a bell ringing in the air.

And I remember when he told me that, something erupted inside of me. I had this strange feeling that I just couldn't place my finger on at the time. I can tell you today what I felt was a joy that I never knew existed. It was a joy that I had been chasing all my life and did not know I was chasing it. And it came down to my purpose, to God's plan for me, that I was finally starting to discover and stepping into.

Connecting with that man in that spot liberated me. I realized that if I want to be in alignment, that meant that I needed to be giving back. That even though I was a drug addict, in drug treatment, with no money and no job, even with all of those facts being stacked against me, I was in a state of being able to help somebody worse off than me.

And there would always be somebody who was worse off than me. There would always be a way for me to give back, no matter what station in life I found myself in. It didn't matter what position I held or who was impressed with what I had achieved, somebody could benefit from getting something from me. It really blew my mind, but it also kind of relaxed me. I had the sense of, *Oh, this is it*. My purpose is to make a difference in this way. My purpose is to contribute. Not just take, take, take.

That led to an epiphany about nature for me. I started looking around at the sky, the trees, the animals, the insects, and I remember thinking about everything that God has created. Everything takes a little and everything gives a little back. This thought was so liberating that it filled up my whole heart. I can say that that was when I committed to a life of service, and that is true. But at the time it was just an indescribable joy I was following.

When I came to that full understanding, I realized I didn't need the big funeral anymore to have a successful life. I didn't need the packed house. Before, I was thinking about the celebrity-style memorial because I was yearning for someone to appreciate me in order to feel worthy. But when you stop and think about it, what was that huge stadium full of adoring fans going to mean to me? I would be dead. I would never have that feeling of knowing that people would mourn my loss. What I was looking for, I would never get.

After that young man came up and talked to me, however, it started a process that lasted a few days and then that stretched into weeks and months. While I was reveling in nature, one of the Bible verses that came back to me was the one that says, "If you love me, feed my sheep." I understood that is what God wanted from me. Despite all the mistakes I'd made and everything I had been through, my time on earth became worthwhile because I had impacted just one life. If I could change just one life, that would be enough. By helping one person, I had met my quota.

Of course, that led to wanting to help more people. It feels nice being nice. It feels good doing good. But now I wanted to make a difference one person at a time, and not for my sake but for the sake of my community, and for society at large. That was very liberating, and to add to that, the impact I could make was directly related to the pain I had gone through in my life. All of that suffering, which I believed was negative, that experience helped me shift my understanding into realizing that my suffering was actually positive. Those issues that used to cause me to walk around with my head down, that burden I had gotten so used to that I didn't even realize I was carrying it, of failures and disappointments and hurt and insufficiencies, it all became worthwhile because it led me to a place to be able to help someone else. Knowing there were no more bad things was empowering and led to a feeling of happiness. If I am doing something, if I am making someone smile, if I am inspiring someone to do great things, I could be content now. Only God knows where that's going to lead, but today, that person has had a better day and I had a role in it.

AFTER THAT, I WOKE UP EVERY DAY AND GOT ON MY KNEES TO PRAY. I ASKED GOD TO continue to give me the strength, the wisdom, and the discernment to do his work. I wanted to make a difference today. I told folks who I met recently that I had been praying for them and I didn't even know it. I was praying so I could have the stamina to do something to make my world a better place, and they were now in that world.

I never prayed for a nice house or nice cars or a great job or a beautiful wife and a lovely family. I never went into anything talking, thinking, or leading with money. Everything that I do have, I never prayed for. What I've found is that if you are doing God's work, if you concentrate on taking care of God's business, he'll end up taking care of your business, and he'll end up doing a much better job than you could ever do. I never had a need that wasn't supplied. There were times when I didn't know how I was going to pay a bill or what-ever, and something popped up when it was supposed to. I stopped worrying about things like that, because I knew the needs would be supplied—maybe not the wants—but the needs would be supplied if there was a commitment to taking care of his business, so I just focused on doing what God wanted me to do. I prayed that I could have a positive impact on other people's lives. That's what I set out to do every single day. I was consumed with that because it was such a great feeling. I didn't know how noble the cause would be; I wasn't at that level yet. All I knew was that I found the purpose for Desmond.

I learned two things in drug treatment that helped me maintain that focus. The first was that the night before, I pick out the clothes I'm going to wear the next day. Then I take my shoes and put them far underneath my bed. That way, in the morning, when I have to get dressed, I have to get on my knees, and since I'm down there already I might as well pray.

The second thing was about the nature of how I prayed. In the church I grew up in, we were taught that God was a fiery God. God was going to cast you into hell and strike you down for sins great and small. You should be very afraid of God, and the more scared you were, the better. What I learned in drug treatment was, that was somebody else's way of prayer. I don't have to pray to God like some-body else prays to God, because that's them, that's their thing; it's not me. If I try to emulate what other people are doing, I may not cover all the things I really need to discuss.

My church growing up made me think I had to be clean to come into the presence of God. What I understood now was that God took you however you were. He wasn't raining down fiery damnation; he loved you exactly as you were.

My way of prayer now became just to have a conversation with God. I didn't have to be perfect to be in a relationship with him. He was more my friend than my adversary—in fact, he was my best friend.

With a best friend, you can tell them anything. That was the mind-set I had when I was on my knees. In the morning, I would talk to him like, *Yo man, God, check this out. I'm messed up, and today, man, this is what's going on.* There was no need to get all flowery about it, to start, "Oh heavenly father . . ." Because then I would get lost in the formalities. I would rather focus on my real needs. I would ask him for wisdom regarding what he wanted me to do, and I would ask him for perseverance to carry out his will.

Simplifying the way I spoke to God also simplified my goals for the day. And if you don't believe in God, that's okay. You can believe in a higher power, or you can just believe in love. You can believe in the power of love, inside you and inside others, to drive you to do better things, to try to make the world better for others. I wanted maybe to learn something new and to make a difference in somebody's life, to help them in some kind of way. That was it, and to not use any drugs. Those were my goals every single day, a basic formula. In the morning, have a conversation with your best friend, and then go out there and just try to do his will, with hopefully enough wisdom and perseverance to last throughout the day and not pick up any drugs. Then come home and call it a day.

FOUR

# A PASSION FOR THE LAW

**N**OW THAT I KNEW I wanted to make a difference in people's lives, I set about trying to figure out the best way to do that. As a little kid growing up, I always wanted to be one of two things: an airplane pilot or a lawyer. My dreams of being a pilot died in the military when I took an eye examination and they determined that I had difficulty focusing on illuminated objects in the dark. You had to have perfect vision to get into flight school, so I ended up as an army helicopter repairman and crewman.

As far as being a lawyer, my childhood idol was Perry Mason. I used to watch that show with my mom; he was my guy. Somewhere along the line, those dreams died, of course, as my drug addiction created an ever bigger barrier to realizing my aspirations. While I was incarcerated, the guy that took over for Perry Mason in my mind was Ben Matlock. Matlock had some serious fees, but there were a lot of times he represented people who could not afford his asking price, folks who just got railroaded by the system or by the police. Matlock became a role model for what I could imagine for myself (especially since there weren't any Black lawyers on TV then). I thought that the better understanding I had of the law, the more useful I could be to people who couldn't pay very much.

The law is so intertwined in all aspects of our lives. Whenever you buy a cell phone, you sign a contract. If you get a traffic ticket, you're dealing with the law. If you buy a home or rent a home—even if you make a purchase at a store—all of that is governed by laws. I wanted to understand the law well enough to help people navigate the different challenges that they may face, and especially because most of the people in my community didn't have lawyers, I saw this as a powerful way to help people.

WHEN I WAS CONVICTED OF POSSESSION OF A FIREARM BY A KNOWN FELON, I THOUGHT my life was over. The judge handed me down a sentence of fifteen years in prison. I got sent to what they call a reception center, which is where they process folks coming into the system. I knew I had to start working on my appeal, but weeks passed, and I didn't hear anything from my attorney, who was a court-appointed public defender. I wrote a couple letters. I tried to make some phone calls. I never received any response, and I started getting very nervous.

I knew you only had a certain period of time in which to file an appeal of your conviction, and that is typically done by the public defender's office. There should have been some type of communication between me and my representative. I couldn't even find out who my public defender was. It was not my initial public defender, because by then my case had been transferred to the appellate division. Somehow I had fallen through the cracks.

Eventually, I decided to take matters into my own hands. I went into the law library at the reception center, asked a few questions, and got some guidance; they actually had law clerks working there to help people like me, which was unusual. I drafted my first legal document, which was a writ of habeas corpus petition for belated appeal.

Basically, it was me writing to the courts, saying, "Hey listen, I know I had a certain amount of time to file the appeal. I know that time has expired, but I have some good reasons why I was unable to file that appeal in a timely way. So because of these reasons, I'm asking you to allow me to file an appeal even though it's late."

Not too long after I submitted that, I received word that my petition was granted. That first document that I drafted got approved by the courts. That was huge for a couple of reasons. Number one, I had never drafted a legal document before—in fact, I hadn't done any writing of any kind since high school, decades previous—so to do so successfully was amazing. But the other thing was, when you're in prison during the appeal process, it's very rare to get the courts to move in your favor.

Once the court granted my petition for belated appeal, they set me up with someone in the public defender's office who specialized in post-conviction appeals. I was already working on my case by the time that attorney was assigned. I had a taste for it now. I was deep in the law books at the library and had come up with about six or seven different grounds for why my conviction should be overturned. Out of the six or seven, I put emphasis on four or five of them. I put all my arguments together and sent it to my lawyer, saying, "Hey, I don't know what you're doing, but this is what I have."

He wrote back, "Okay, great. We'll work together and make sure that we're in communication with each other."

When my attorney filed his initial brief, he chose to put emphasis on one thing that I didn't even think had a shot: an argument around the selection of the jury. But that was the thing that got me free. My case actually made the law books, so it's printed case material that people cite to this day. That is how I ended up being released after three years instead of having to serve the full fifteen-year term.

WHEN MY FIRST PETITION IN PRISON WAS GRANTED, WORD GOT OUT. A FAVORABLE ruling was news on the inside. You can imagine the number of people that were coming to me, asking me to work on their case.

I didn't work on many, but every case that I worked on when I was incarcerated received some type of favorable response from the court. I guess that made me kind of valuable there. If there were inmates who had an issue with me or wanted to fight me, there would always be some key person who stepped in and said, "You're not gonna mess with that dude. That's my lawyer." I think that helped my experience in prison not be as violent as it could have been. I was afforded some degree of protection. If I got sent to confinement, I wouldn't be able to continue working on anyone's case, so naturally there were some folks who were invested in me not getting into any trouble.

I remember one case in particular where the gentleman was convicted of possession of cocaine. This guy was really cool, like quite a few of the guys that I met on the inside. You could see that deep down inside—as opposed to the broad brush that all convicts get painted with—he was a nice person, really down to earth. He just had a problem with drugs. I noticed that with the overwhelming majority of folks I met when I was incarcerated; they were either under the influence of drugs at the time they committed the crime, or they were trying to get drugs when they were caught. This was one of those guys who, if you took away his drug addiction, could have been your neighbor, and a good neighbor at that.

Anyway, he was caught with a small amount of cocaine and was sentenced to a few years. When he approached me, he told me how it wasn't him. He didn't have the cocaine. He was just a passenger in the car. I shrugged that off; there is a running joke that everybody's innocent in prison. But then he asked me to look at his case, and I decided to do it because I thought he was an all-right guy. When I read the transcript of his trial, I noticed something in one of the officers' testimonies that stuck out. It was when he was describing a broken taillight. I remembered some months back when I was in the law library reading trial cases and came across a similar story. I looked up the case, and sure enough, the cases were basically identical. In the printed case, an officer had used a standard traffic stop to pull someone over. But in his testimony, he articulated that when he approached the defendant's car, he noticed the light emanating from the broken taillight. So the light bulb was still operable, but the taillight assembly was cracked. And that was enough to let the defendant in the law books off the charge, and it worked for my guy as well.

It was a technicality, sure. But I never had an issue with using anything in the purview of the law to help someone, especially when the odds were stacked so high against Black and Brown people or underserved communities in general. There are certain parts of town where they don't run routine traffic stops. Or if they do pull someone over for a missing taillight, it's with a smile and a wave and a *Don't forget to get that checked out* as opposed to *Hands where I can see them* and a full search of the car. If the police were to search every car with a missing taillight, you never know what they might find. But as countless reports have shown, you're much more likely to be pulled over for driving-while-Black then for actually having a taillight out, and the consequences are much heavier if you are a person of color, and far worse if you have a criminal record.

None of this has changed, by the way. I remember getting pulled over during the campaign for the ballot initiative, and it was a traumatizing experience. The police officer approached my car with his hands on his gun. He had pulled me over for nothing; he made some excuse about the car, but it was a rental car. There was nothing odd about the car. I know that even after I've changed my life around, every time I get pulled over there is going to be a heightened interaction, an encounter that I might not emerge from fairly.

What that leads to in our society are good men and women languishing on the inside for years. Typically, when somebody goes to prison, the main places they hang out are the rec yard, the dorms, or in the weight pile lifting weights. They resign themselves to having to do their time and go about trying to adapt to prison life instead. You wake up, do your chores, and go to your job, or you're out in the yard walking around. In Florida, we have blue prison uniforms. I remember looking at the people, thinking we were just a bunch of blue cows grazing in the grass.

There are so many people out there lifting weights, but when you walk into the library, you can count the people in there on your fingers. Some prisons don't even have complete libraries; you have to write for the materials that you want and then wait and try to keep your momentum up on your own in the meantime. Other libraries are very small or have outdated casebooks. Your access is handicapped, and that cuts into the desire or willpower for people to actually go and work on their case.

There was one case in particular where I helped some law clerks with a young man . . . well, he was young when he came to prison at the age of seventeen. At that time, he had just fallen right into the routine of being a blue cow grazing. In fact, he had done fifteen years before he asked somebody to look at something in his case. When we did, we found out he should have never been incarcerated. He ended up going home, but thinking about how he wasted a decade and a half of his life makes me cry every time.

When I wasn't in the law library in prison, I worked as a math tutor. It was another way to help people. Everyone who goes into prison is given an exam. Your reading and math scores determine where they place you for employment, whether you get a job like custodian or cutting the grass or can do something of more substance. If I could help inmates raise certain scores, they could stop working in menial roles like digging ditches, which could also help raise their self-esteem. They were appreciative of me for that.

Monday through Friday, I would go to the classroom with other prisoners and help them master mathematics, not for the GED or any external educational purpose but to get them to a point where they were able to score high enough on the math section to get a better job inside the prison. I would sit in the front of a room full of students, and when people had problems, they would come up to me and ask my help in certain areas.

I remember one day I was looking at this guy. He would not come up to ask me for help, but I could see that he was struggling and getting frustrated. Finally, I decided to approach him and ask him what was wrong. His name was Cedric. He told me, "Man, I never could get these fractions." It was frustrating him.

I told him to follow me to my desk, where we could have some privacy. I asked him what he was incarcerated for. As it turns out, he was a mid-level drug dealer, not necessarily the guy who was on the corner but definitely not the guy bringing in the kilos; he was somewhere in between.

I asked him, "If you have a kilo of cocaine and you have four friends that you want to break off and give some work to, how would you do it?"

He said, "Man, I'd break them into quarters," and he got very animated, explaining the drug trade to me. "Not everybody's going to be equal though. Some people are going to have more connections or work harder. So, I might give one guy a half, and one guy a quarter, and two other guys an eighth each." He was able to actually put the whole system together.

At the end I told him, "Bro, you just did math. You just did fractions."

That taught me something important. You have these standardized tests that supposedly measure a person's intelligence or propensity to learn. But in reality, different people come from different environments. If you put someone in an environment they're not familiar with, they'll think they're stupid. When they come to understand the core concepts, on the other hand, because they're in the right environment, one would see an increase in their confidence level.

I decided that I was going to continue to teach this man math using the drug trade. When we got to the lesson about negative and positive integers, I gave him the example where he just fronted someone a kilo of cocaine.

"How much are you charging him?" I asked.

"Eighteen thousand dollars."

"So, is he eighteen thousand dollars to the good or to the bad?"

Cedric said, "Oh, that's eighteen thousand dollars to the bad."

I said, "That's eighteen thousand dollars. Now, if a week later the guy gives you nine thousand dollars, what's his status?"

"Oh, he's only nine thousand dollars to the bad, now . . . so negative nine thousand dollars?"

After that he was able to work with integers and divide and multiply, positive or negative, it didn't matter. The interesting thing about Cedric was that I had seen him before. He was in my dorm. When I first noticed him, it was because you couldn't help but notice him. He was a very loud and boisterous person. He walked around with his pants hanging low, his hair looking crazy, and a mouth full of gold teeth. He had this rough voice and would always act like he was mad at the world.

What I noticed was that every time we successfully completed a section of math, it was almost like a layer was peeled away from him. Eventually he got to the point that he was getting ready to take his GED. He had already elevated past the occupational testing by this point. Now when you looked at him, he was more clean-cut, pants on his waist with a belt, talking in a normal tone of voice, and walking around with a smile on his face.

I was able to witness a transformation in this man. At the beginning of our relationship he talked about how when he got out he was going to tighten up his game in the drug trade. Now he was talking about how he could have a different way of life when he was released, and he could see himself doing other things, even entrepreneurship.

As I saw this new Cedric emerging, it really hit home that a lot of these guys who were incarcerated had these macho tendencies, but it was all a façade. When you peel away those layers, what you find inside is a scared boy who was told that he would never amount to anything, so he suppressed those insecurities with this sense of bravado. If they don't do well on a standardized test, they get labeled remedial, and no one expects them to go to college or be successful. If they want a job where they can make good money, they're not thinking they can be a doctor or a lawyer. They're thinking the only profession open to them is dope boy. That's the way to get the clothes and the car and the girls.

Someone who is in that situation puts on layers to protect his insecurities and at the same time minimizes the importance of education. The guy that's smart, we call a nerd or a square and belittle him so we won't feel as bad. At the same time, because deep down inside we don't feel significant, we need to become more aggressive. We can't let somebody try us. We can't let anybody see that we're soft. We end up fighting because someone stepped on our tennis shoes or shooting someone over a trivial dispute. But the whole time, we just want to feel like we are *somebody*. We just want to be loved. That was me, as well. I saw some of myself in Cedric. That experience with him planted a seed in me that would eventually bloom a few years later. As much as I enjoyed helping someone else become more successful, to really tap into their inner potential, I couldn't hide behind that forever. The time would come when I would have to step out.

# FIVE

# BACK TO SCHOOL

W HEN IT WAS GETTING CLOSE for me to finish drug treatment, I started thinking about what the rest of my life would look like. One of the things that stood out, my most pressing need, was that I did not want to use drugs anymore. You use drugs, you get to a low point in your life, you stop, your life improves, and then at some point you relapse; you go back to using drugs and you get to an even lower place, and that cycle just keeps going on and on, further down and down. I was tired of that vicious cycle.

I wanted to figure out what I could do to raise my self-esteem, to give myself hope, to the point where I would never have to end up at those railroad tracks again. When I thought about what led me there, what really opened up those floodgates, it was the passing of my mother. I always used to have two fears. Fear number one was that I was going to die without having anyone to carry on my name; I was going to die without having a son. Fear number two was that my mother would die before me. I loved my mom so much, I just could not imagine going on living without her.

When she did pass away, in 1997, I took it as hard as expected. I was already using drugs, but after her death I really dove into my abuse. I sold things out of my mom's house to sustain my habit. Most of the rear wall of the structure, particularly in the dining room area, had what they call jalousie windows: windows with a bunch of thin slats that you can twist and roll out and roll in. They were made out of aluminum, and I sold that metal to buy crack. At some point in my addiction, I had actually dismantled everything to the point where there was no back wall to the house. I shared that story with people at drug treatment facilities. I told them that's when I really became a rock star, because my dining room became a stage. It was like I was an artist performing for the world.

Eventually, I was the cause of our losing our mom's house altogether. In six months, I was able to dismantle it and lose it through foreclosure because of my drug addiction. I destroyed what she worked her whole life for. From her early days, working as a maid in San Juan, Puerto Rico, or a waitress in Saint Croix, she had worked herself to the bone to have a home. What a way to honor her life and legacy!

So as I was contemplating my next steps after drug treatment, I started thinking about education. Throughout my life, my mother had always stressed to me the value of getting an education. She was always putting me in book clubs and things of that nature. I used to think about her while I was in prison, helping tutor fellow prisoners on the math section of the employment exam. I felt like I would be making my mother proud if she knew what I was doing. She told me people can take a lot of things from you, but they can never take your education.


IN DOWNTOWN MIAMI THERE WAS AN ABOVE-RAIL SHUTTLE SYSTEM CALLED THE METRO Mover that a lot of homeless people used to use, because it was free and a very convenient mode of transportation. I would ride it from Chapman Partnership to various points around the Brickell Avenue area. Along that route were two places that I loved to stop. Number one was the courthouse, where they had a law library; I would go in there to read cases. Another place where I stopped frequently was the Wolfson Campus of Miami Dade College. Every now and then, I would also go to the library there to go online and just do some research or find out what was going on around the world.

I used to watch the college kids going back and forth, and I imagined what it would be like if I were actually in school. I never thought at the time that it would be a real possibility. There have been so many points in my life when I was living in the homeless shelter, and even prior to that when I was on the streets, that I would have these wish-fulfillment scenarios. I would be walking somewhere and see a nice house and think, "Wow, it sure would be nice to live in a house like that." I would watch people driving to and from work while I was walking or catching the bus and wonder what that kind of freedom felt like, just to be able to leave your house when you wanted to, and take any route you chose to get to your destination.

Those were the kinds of feelings I'd have when I walked by Miami Dade, but I always dismissed them because here I was, a convicted felon and a homeless person. The college was in downtown Miami where a lot of the homeless people congregate, but it wasn't antiquated. The campus consisted of modern buildings; they were constantly expanding it and building out. Right now, with all eight campuses included, Miami Dade is one of the largest colleges in the country. If I furthered my education, I could both honor my mother and help raise my self-esteem so I wouldn't be as tempted to relapse. *You know what?* I thought. *Maybe I can go back to school.*

I didn't think I was going to be able to get in, but on one of those days when I was just roaming endlessly around, I decided to stop into the admissions department and give it a shot. I had to fill out an application. Now, mind you, I had never applied to a college or a university in my life. From high school, I went straight into the military. I always envisioned it to be such an arduous process, so I was kind of shocked by how easy it was. It wasn't a matter of waiting for an acceptance letter or anything. You just applied and you were good to go.

I had to take an exam to see where they should place me. Again, I got nervous, but it was much easier than I expected. I was always a kid who tested well. In the army, I did great on the test we called the ASVAB (Armed Services Vocational Aptitude Battery). I had it all worked out: I was going to be II Bravo Infantry, and then from infantry, I was going to airborne school in Italy. Then, after airborne school, I was going to go to ranger school, and then I'd be Rambo.

At the time I took the ASVAB, I had a girlfriend whose parents were blown away by how well I did. They told me, "Wait a minute, why would you go into the infantry, when you have these amazing

scores? You should be going to West Point; you should be an officer."
What they really meant was, *You need to be an officer, because if you're
going to be with our daughter, you've got to be able to provide for her.*

That discussion caused my goal to shift from wanting to be another Rambo to now becoming a pilot. Eventually, when I wasn't able
to pass the eye test, I switched my sights on being an interpreter for
military intelligence. I passed a very difficult test that was actually in a
made-up language you had to decipher. It was like learning a foreign
language right on the spot, but I could do it.

That was all many years before, however. Had I lost some of my
natural intelligence during my years of drug abuse and life on the
streets when I wasn't sleeping or eating properly or doing the things
that contribute to being able to keep all of my faculties? I thought I
was still doing okay, and I had a way that I knew.

Are you ready for this? When I was homeless, I always remembered that Bill Clinton did a lot of crossword puzzles. So I would manage to get the day's paper, and I would do the crossword puzzle. If I
was able to get at least three-quarters complete, I knew I wasn't losing
my mind. That was my gauge. That was my daily test of making sure
I wasn't losing it.

WHEN MY TEST RESULTS CAME BACK, THE COLLEGE LET ME KNOW THAT I DIDN'T HAVE TO
take any remedial classes. I could just get going. What did I want
to study?

I reviewed the different courses that were offered, and the program that seemed to call to me the loudest was paralegal studies. Ever
since I had worked on my own appeal process, and through helping
other inmates with their cases, my interest in the law had been re-
awakened. Paralegal studies seemed to be a natural fit and an area
where I felt that I had a good chance of doing well. I thought that if
I could use the skills that I learned while I was in prison, combined
with my affinity for reading, I could get a respectable, decent job.

I was not thinking about going to law school at that point, or even
eventually being a lawyer someday. That was way too much. *Maybe* I
could be a paralegal and be able to assist an attorney in various cases.
Someday.

I remember my first day in class. I got there early because I wanted to sit at the front so I didn't miss anything. In my head, I thought, *Hey, I'm an older person. I've got all these young kids that I'm going to be in class with, and they probably have the edge on me because they are coming straight from high school.* I'd been away from school for a long time, so I wanted to make sure that I caught everything the teacher was saying. I didn't want to be in a row farther back, because I didn't want someone dropping a pencil, or talking to classmates, or flirting with a girl to distract me from learning. I established my seat in the front row, and that was where I always sat thereafter.

One of my favorite parts of orientation when you start a new class is finding out the office hours of the professors. I was one of those guys who believed in using that time. I don't think I had one professor who I did not go visit during office hours, so I could be better, so I could find out more about whatever assignments I was working on. And I would always be ahead of schedule on my assignments. Whenever I got work assigned to me, I would start on it right then and there. I didn't wait and put it off and come back to it later on, because I knew things could happen, and then when I was in that time crunch, I wasn't going to actually produce my best work. I believed in getting ahead of the game.

I was looking to learn as much as possible. But I was also terrified that the school was going to come to me one day and say, "I'm sorry, Desmond, we made a mistake by letting you in." Maybe it would be the financial aid people who would eventually discover exactly who I was and my criminal history. Or someone else in the administration would say, "We cannot have an ex-drug addict or someone who is currently living at a homeless shelter matriculated here. He must have slipped through the cracks somehow."

This thought occurred too many times during my school years. While I was sitting there, I used to think, *Man, these people don't know who they have in their classroom. I wonder if they know that I'm a crack-head. I've been in prison, homeless.* . . . . I was waiting for them to chase me out of the classroom.

My goal then was to be able to prove, when somebody raised an issue about my past, that I was worthy. I wanted to be able to have something to prove that I deserved an opportunity to get an education.

So I set out to get straight A's. And for the most part, that's what I did. There were three classes where I didn't get an A. Every other one of my sixty credits for my associate's degree had an A next to it on my transcript. My thinking was that if I could just do the best that I possibly could, then, when these people eventually did come and get me, I could say, "Hey, I know I'm not supposed to be here, but look what I've done since you let me in. Give me a chance. Make an exception."

But that time never came. It's truly a testament to that system that an older Black man with a criminal record, a man living in a shelter and unable to pay tuition, was nonetheless allowed—even encouraged—to attend college and to excel at it. Sadly, it doesn't happen everywhere or for everyone, but a high school and college education should be a basic right for everyone living in this country, no matter what hurdles they face.

I totally dedicated myself to being the best that I could possibly be, and I think my professors noticed that. The funny thing is, I had that commitment even back when I was a drug addict, albeit in a misguided direction.

When I was first introduced to crack cocaine, I was shown how to smoke it out of a soda can or a beer can, where to poke the holes and where the ashes go, how the device is fashioned. That was a really crude way of smoking, and I had a natural desire to find out a better way, because, of course, I wanted to inhale all of the smoke that I possibly could.

I graduated from a can to a glass pipe. Somebody had to teach me that, but then I went home and tried to improve on what they taught me by experimentation. I ended up learning something new about the residue that you can bring back together so you can stretch your drugs.

I was always searching. I really became a student of getting high. How could I get the best high possible? I was committed to finding that out. That commitment didn't just stop with trying to learn the best way to smoke; it was also about getting the best drug. I remember riding a bike in the middle of a hurricane, just so I could buy a crack rock from a good location. I wanted the best, and I was willing to do anything to get it.

If I was that committed to something that destroyed my life, then what type of commitment should I have to do something that would improve my life, like being in college? I figured that I need to put forth at least the same degree of effort. If I actually worked harder to destroy my life than to save my life, then I wasn't on the right road to healing. If I could have an even stronger commitment to improving my life than to destroying it, then I could really, fully, and finally be proud of myself.

And that is what I did. My first year, I worked incredibly hard and was invited to apply for the honors society, Phi Beta Kappa. When I got accepted, that lifted up my self-esteem tremendously. I'm an honors student! Then other offers started coming in to join this or that academic fraternity. I ended up being a member of three of them in total and got to wear their stoles when I graduated two years later with my associate's degree with highest honors and as the honors recipient for our paralegal program.

# SIX

# STAYING SOBER

OBVIOUSLY, IT'S EASIER to study and get good grades when you're sober. It's easier to remember things. Everything's easier. As important as my education was to me, I could not place anything above my recovery. I was very, very strict. I would not engage in anything that was considered a threat to my recovery. I did not want anything in my life that would be a distraction.

Every day at the treatment center, a different person would come to the meeting. It's generally the same set of people that come every week, but they bring guest speakers with them so they don't have to speak all the time. So you knew that on a certain day, for example, John was coming. John always brought doughnuts. Then on a certain day, Brian would come. Brian wouldn't bring anything but his problems. Whether it was his girlfriend or his job, Brian would just complain to us and his complaints were starting to get me worried. *Man,* I thought, *if life is going to be this depressing, I don't know if I'm going to be able to stay away from drugs forever.*

Then this guy Frank H. came in, and he was like a breath of fresh air, a crazy, fun-loving Cuban American who I would eventually consider my brother. Frank's thing was to bring pizza, but he brought so much more than that—he brought his full self. He told crazy stories that made people laugh, but there was always a message there and he had a commitment to staying clean. Frank was an exciting, adventurous, daring guy, who was at the same time fully committed to whoever needed his help. I've seen him take the shoes off his feet to give to someone who didn't have any and go home barefoot! He not only came to our meetings, but he would take meetings to different treatment centers. Later I would model myself after Frank when I tried to both make the most out of life and be there for other folks.

Frank played the role of sponsor in my life as well. Eventually, he even opened up his house to me and allowed me to come live with him, his wife, and kids. He had a room there that he would rent. I eventually met his entire family, and they took me in like I was their family as well. His mom really loved me. Every time she saw me, she would grab my face and give me a big kiss, just like a Cuban mom would. I remember when the hurricane came through and destroyed Frank's parents' house and they had to live in a trailer, we went to make sure their awning was extended correctly. I was also there when his dad passed away. Slowly but surely my friendship with Frank turned into a brotherhood. We were kindred spirits.

Leaving the homeless shelter was a definite step forward for my self-esteem. Then Frank had the idea to take the house behind his and open it as a three-quarter-way house. The difference between a three-quarter-way house and a halfway house is that a three-quarter-way house is geared toward people who are recovering from substance addiction. It's a different environment. A halfway house is something that the government might run for folks who are coming out of prison so that they can transition back into mainstream society. It's more correction themed. The three-quarter-way house has more of a recovery theme. Our folks had to go to meetings.

Frank asked me if I wanted to be the manager, and so that's what I did. My life was living in a home full of recovering addicts. We had either three or four people bunking together, depending on the size of the room—between ten and fifteen people total in the house at one time. Personally, I had two other roommates with me. Everyone in the house was a recovering addict. I made sure that everybody went to their mandatory meetings and that they did their assigned chores.

I got to see all the different personalities of an addict. I got to see all of the different tricks that people try to play, their cunning or their passive aggression or their outright hostility. I got to see the type of impact that drugs and alcohol had on different folks coming from different places. We had people ranging from a person from the street to a professional golfer living in our house. We had people of all colors and ethnicities, we had teachers, we had attorneys—drugs and alcohol don't discriminate.

BEING THE MANAGER OF THE THREE-QUARTER-WAY HOUSE WAS A GREAT LEARNING experience for me that really helped me deepen my understanding of addiction. For one thing, it created a level of accountability. When I was leading meetings, I might think I was talking to other people, but I was really talking to myself. In my head, I was talking to try to share my experience, strength, and hope with the folks at the treatment center and let them know that they could make it, but what I realized was that whatever I shared with clients ended up applying to my own life.

When I was able to bring up things that happened to me in my past, I was able to actually confront those things, and in confronting those things, I came to find out that even though they happened *to* me, that didn't necessarily mean that they *defined* me, that I was a bad person. Before I would suppress the memory of bad events because I held the belief that I was the one who brought it on. Bad events meant I was a bad person, and because I was a bad person, I didn't deserve happiness or love. When we're dealing with our recovery, we have to find ways to approach those issues, the parts of our past that suggest we don't deserve to be successful. Being able to uncover and confront the darkest parts of my history, I was not only able to engage in an important conversation with others; I was able to convince myself that I had a right to live and even to succeed.

The world will get you. You need to have a philosophy that will keep you clean and sober over the years. Otherwise, if you get laid off from your job, you're going to go to the dope, or if you break up with your girlfriend or you have a death in the family or there's some kind of personal trauma or conflict . . . the dope will always be waiting for you.

It's a battle between our subconscious and our conscious minds. You know how we've read books that say we're only using about 10 percent of our brain's capacity? I equate that with consciousness; our conscious mind represents around 10 percent of everything that transpires in our being. Your 10 percent might be saying that you don't want to pick up drugs anymore, but your 90 percent is saying, Yes, I do want to get high. Because your head is a democratic place, that's what happens. The majority rules.

There is just so much that's going on in our subconscious minds. Consciously, as an addict, I do not want to destroy my life. I want to live, I want to love, I want to be loved. That won't turn the tide, however, if subconsciously I hate myself. Then, in spite of what comes out of my mouth to you, I'm going to end up doing something destructive.

The key is figuring out how to get the majority in your head to tell you that you want to live. When I kept going with my recovery, I kept going within myself, and I kept finding more garbage that was inside me, more issues that needed to be worked out, won over, so that the majority of me could say: Desmond deserves to live. Desmond deserves to be loved. Desmond deserves to be happy.

DID EVERYONE THAT I SUPPORTED MAKE IT THROUGH? NO, AND IT'S THE SAME THING with recidivism for people who've been in prison. Some of the addicts I mentored got to the other side, and some of them died. Addiction is one of the most harrowing trials a human being can undergo.

From 2006 to 2012, I lived in a house full of drug addicts and alcoholics, so I got to see this ordeal on a daily basis, twenty-four hours a day, seven days a week. I know there's more to recovery than just willpower. I've seen people cry, just break down. They don't want to get high, they don't. They really don't. They try really hard, but they end up relapsing.

It was almost impossible to watch at certain times. One of the things I used to think about to keep myself sane was those television shows when someone's in a coma. The body has shut down so it can heal itself, and you might hear a doctor in the program utter a line like, "We've done all we can." It's now up to that individual to heal. When you look at the human body, you can plainly see it is one of God's greatest creations. For this machine to function the way it does is a miracle. When someone is very sick, the body has a mechanism to heal itself that is outside of what another human could initiate or control. We have to trust that the body has everything it needs.

In a similar way, I think the answers to our questions are located inside of us. That's that secret place of the most high. It's not in a building; it's within us, because that's where God is. After a certain point in recovery, it's not about willpower. It's about how do we tap into our innermost selves, our innermost souls, and deal with what's inside of there? That's where we need to look.

And sometimes we get to see that beautiful miracle unfolding. Frank and I used to take meetings at different treatment centers around the county. Some folks would get attracted to the message one of us would bring, and when they were getting ready to graduate from their program and were looking for a three-quarter-way house to slowly ease their way back into their family's life, guys would give us a call from time to time and ask to live at the recovery house.

There was this one guy, Louis. When he came to us, I remember he had to walk everywhere he went. From walking, he got a bike. Then he got a moped. Then he got a car. Then he was going to school. I don't want to give myself too much credit, but he told me he was basically following in my footsteps. Now Louis is a successful sound engineer in the movie industry. Did I give him his ear for music? Of course not. Did I give him his initiative? I can't claim that either. But I was proud to provide a supportive environment while he got his subconscious mind in line with his conscious mind so that everything was working together for the best interests of Louis.

IN RECOVERY, RELAPSES DON'T JUST HAPPEN. YOU ARE EITHER ENGAGING IN A SERIES OF behaviors that strengthen your conscious mind and confront your subconscious, or you are priming yourself for a relapse. You can control the structure and the system you have internally better than you could ever control external forces. Life-changing events will come out of nowhere and slap you right in the face, and your first reaction could be to drink or get high. I had one of those.

It was called the Spider-Man Massacre. Some armed home invaders came to a child's birthday party in North Miami–Dade and held them hostage. The gunmen mistakenly thought that there was a safe full of money inside the house. But those people were my family and friends. They shot one of my nieces and my other niece's two children.

One of the armed robbers told everyone he would have no trouble killing them if they didn't give him what he wanted. He chased them out of the house, shooting at them. A close friend of the family and her son were shot to death.

When I found out what happened, I was on my way to a meeting with Frank.

He asked me, "Do you want to go to the hospital?"

Initially, I thought about going to the hospital. Family members could be clinging to life, and other family members were probably rushing there worried out of their minds. At the same time, I could see a relapse looming. So I was left with a choice: I could either go and be with my family amid the uncertainty of how I was going to respond to the crisis, or I could go to a safe place to protect my sobriety.

I said, "There's nothing I can do. No, let's go take this meeting first."

That is huge in recovery. When tragic things happen, we make choices. In the past, we made choices to pick up. Now, I knew the best choice for me, despite whatever happened to the family, was to make sure I got to a meeting. I needed to be grounded. Then after the meeting, I could go to the hospital.

My niece and the two children of my other niece who were shot survived. They were shot in the head and the arm. One of them is now a criminal justice major in college, and the other one is a budding youth pastor.

FROM THE DEPTHS OF TRAGEDY TO THE HEIGHTS OF JOY, RECOVERY HAD IT ALL IN store for me.

Frank had jet skis, and one day he invited me to go jet skiing with him. We went to a lake by Miami International Airport. The lakes in Florida are dark, and I tried to explain to Frank why I wasn't too keen on our plan.

Of all the movies I saw when I was a little kid, *Jaws* scared me the most. That movie terrified me for the rest of my life. As a kid, when I would be in the tub, playing Tarzan or whatever, I would start thinking about *Jaws*, and making that *Jaws* sound, and then all the fun would be over. I'd be ready to hop out of that bath because I was too scared to stay in there any longer. Even knowing that would happen, I would always do that.

Well, the thing that topped *Jaws* was alligators. In Florida, alligators are everywhere. I just knew that no matter what body of water I might be looking at, there was an alligator lurking in there somewhere, waiting to eat me. Add to that the fact that I had never been on a jet ski before and this just turned into a very bad idea. Somehow, though, Frank convinced me to get on a jet ski by myself. I was so scared as we were put-putting out onto the lake. The only thing I was thinking was, *Whatever you do, Desmond, don't fall. There are alligators in there, waiting on you.*

I was out there, casually put-putting around while Frank got on his jet ski and went zooming right by me, creating waves. I screamed at him, "Leave me alone! Don't make me fall!"

I got into the middle of the lake, but Frank kept circling around me. He said, "I'm going to keep on doing this until you ride this jet ski the right way."

He wanted me to overcome my fear. So I started opening up the jet ski a little bit, and then a little bit more. Gliding over the water, I thought, *Man, this feels all right. . . . Okay, this is cool.*

Pretty soon I started going faster and making waves just slightly. Eventually, I decided to open it all the way up until I was bouncing off all these waves and screaming at the top of my lungs. "Wooooohooooooooooo!"

All of a sudden, it hit me like a wall—bam—I had to stop. It blew my mind, because that was the first time that I was actually having fun and didn't have to be drunk or high. That was a life-changing moment. That was the first time I realized I could actually have a happy life without being intoxicated or under the influence of drugs. I started to cry, thinking back on my life and how the good times always seemed like they had to include some kind of substance. It was a transformational moment for me.

When that moment passed, I started riding again. Within minutes, however, the one thing I feared most happened: I fell off the jet ski! Oh my god, I was so terrified! I was scrambling to get back on the jet ski but didn't know how, and I knew that at any moment this alligator is coming to get me. I finally made it back on, and I did not fall off again that day. But what I did know is that it was an amazing experience. I knew it for a fact, from that day on, that I didn't have to get high anymore. But I didn't get over the alligator thing.

# SEVEN

# COMMUNITY SERVICE IS
# MY LOTTERY TICKET

**M**Y LIFE IN THOSE DAYS WAS FULL, between managing the three-quarter-way house where I lived and going to school. I wasn't a person who slept eight hours a night in those days. There would be times where I'd have to get up at three o'clock in the morning to get some reading or writing done, especially as I chose to continue my education after I earned my associate's degree to pursue a full-fledged bachelor's degree.

At the same time, I knew that I couldn't put anything ahead of my sobriety. I was still running meetings at our place and taking meetings to treatment centers. It was maybe a 50/50 balance between education and recovery, so when the opportunity came along to get into advocacy, I didn't know what side of that 50/50 ratio that work was going to fit into. At the same time, I knew I couldn't turn it down.

The first organization I joined was called the Homeless/Formerly Homeless Forum. The primary focus of this organization was to advocate for sensible policies that would create more affordable housing for individuals and for programs that would help reduce the homeless population in Miami-Dade County. It was led by people who were recovering addicts, people who had experienced homelessness, or people who might have been incarcerated. That felt like an ideal fit for me to begin my advocacy work because I was a combination of all three.

The person who had the most influence over me from that organization was Pauline Trotman. Pauline had walked a lot of the steps that I had, including being homeless, even though she was further down the activist path than me. She treated the people we served as if she were one of them, which she had been. She never forgot where she came from. From sleeping in cars and abandoned buildings, she managed to rise to a very prominent position within the homeless advocacy and recovery community in South Florida, and she continues to be a constant guiding force today.

Pauline used to say that having gone from homeless to homeowner meant that anything was possible. She wanted to make sure that opportunity existed for others. Helping with that organization to get people off the streets, helping them find a safe place to live, made me feel like I was doing something good. I knew that all of a person's struggles are related and that homelessness can be at the root of so many of a person's problems.

When you're homeless, it's a hustle. This is not an indictment of people living without permanent homes, because you have a lot of folks who are out there through no fault of their own. They could have fallen victim to a bad economy or been part of a family that was turned out into the street. During my time on the streets, I ran across brilliant people who had fallen on hard times without any support system: doctors, lawyers, teachers. You'd be surprised at the wide range of people who live without permanent housing, at least for part of their lives; they include people of all races and ethnicities, of all socioeconomic backgrounds, from many varied backgrounds.

But when you are homeless, you're susceptible to committing a certain number of crimes each year. In Dade County around the turn of the century, the average number of crimes committed by a homeless person a year was 90. Think about that: just to survive, you will commit 90 crimes within a year's time. If you're homeless with a substance abuse problem, that number shoots up to about 150 crimes a year.

When you're out on the streets, you increase the likelihood of interaction with law enforcement as well. I've been arrested for shoplifting and for possession of drugs and for possession of paraphernalia. There are times when I would get arrested for something I wasn't even guilty of. I'd go to jail and be offered an opportunity to take a plea. The state prosecutor would offer me credit for time served. That means that if you take their plea, you can go home that day. I didn't have a home to go to, but I had drugs to get to. And so, I would take a plea, adding to my criminal record, so I could get back out to use drugs.

I was mounting up the convictions, which eventually comes back and haunts you. That was the case with the charge that got me into prison. One of my prior convictions, as the result of a plea, made me a felon and was used as a qualifying offense, what they call a predicate, for state prosecutors to be able to charge me with possession of a firearm by a convicted felon.

The story of that night went like this: I was in the home of a friend where I was squatting. Late that night, there was a heavy banging on the door that startled me. When I got up and looked out the window, I saw a lot of men in all black. My first thought was that these guys were coming to rob us.

Then I heard, "Police! Open up! Police!"

I went and opened the door and when I did that, the police dragged me outside and laid me on the ground, facedown. There were other people who were pulled out of the house as well. Then, they searched the home. While they were searching, they found a gun.

I didn't know this at the time, but the owner of the house was there as well that night, hanging out. He had other homes, but he was actually there that night. While they were searching the house, he was lying next to me.

I remember whispering to him, "You need to ask them if they have a search warrant."

Eventually he did ask them. They asked him if he was the owner, and when he said yes, they picked him up and brought him into the house with them. Several minutes later they all came back out, made me stand up, and handcuffed me. When I got in the car, they told me I was being arrested for illegal possession of a firearm.

The police later reported that they were driving down the street and heard a woman scream. That made them stop their car, get out, and go onto the property where we were. They said they looked in our window and saw me standing in a bedroom with a gun in my hand. That was the story they used for probable cause. The reality was, police found the gun in a cupboard in the kitchen, and the gun belonged to the owner of the house. He wasn't the legal owner of the gun, though; it was the registered firearm of his cousin, who was in the military and had given it to him.

Apparently, when police found the gun, they explained to the owner of the house that somebody had to go to jail and who was it going to be. Now, I have never owned a firearm. Throughout my life in the streets, I've come across them in various ways, but I've never been the person to just be carrying around a firearm. As a former military person, I have great respect for the damage it can do. But the owner of the house decided to name me as the owner of the gun.

He later told me that he figured better me than him, because at least he had money to bail me out. Which was fine reasoning, except with my list of prior convictions it meant my entire life changed in an instant.


THE MORE COMFORTABLE I GOT AT MIAMI DADE COLLEGE, THE MORE I OPENED UP TO other students about my past. I became a student assistant in the paralegal program's administration, which was headquartered in a place called the Law Center. My role was to help students, not only to decide what they wanted to do in their college career but to serve as a mentor and counselor for those who chose to enter the paralegal program. I was always there to hand out advice, whether it was about their classes or life in general. I heard about their struggles with their boyfriends or girlfriends, or their families, or their living conditions. Some of these kids were young enough to be my daughters or my sons, and I tried to give them some of the benefit of my experience.

I used to talk to the students at the college about these homeless people they saw roaming around the campus. I could remember how, before that happened to me, when I saw a homeless person I would just conveniently turn away. Or, if I did pay that person any attention, it wasn't positive attention. I would be thinking, *That person is never going to amount to anything.*

When I shared my story of being homeless with the students, I would challenge them to look at the homeless population differently:

instead of seeing someone as a hopeless case or a pariah or a drain on our community, look at the person as someone who could be the next Desmond or even better. "I was once that person," I would tell them.

I started to realize early on that I actually had the power to help shift the narrative and cause people to look at things differently, in a way that would, in turn, make our community a little bit better. Some of the students could relate because they had come from a background where something similar had happened to someone they knew. No matter what crowd I'm in, I often find people who have been through the same thing I have or have a family member or close friend who has struggled with addiction and sometimes homelessness as well.

Eventually, I revealed my story to my professors, opening up about what I had gone through. Up until then, only people in recovery knew who Desmond really was. Everybody else just saw a guy who was smiling all the time and trying to be helpful. They didn't know the backstory. They didn't know that a lot of my happiness was due to the fact that I couldn't believe I was in college, and I was grateful for the opportunity to do something with my life other than using drugs and being homeless. Eventually, my story made its way to the president of the college, who was amazed by what I had gone through. I had come a long way from being afraid that my secret was going to come out and that I would be hauled out of class one day. Yes, I was being accepted now. Yes, my story was inspirational, but did it only apply to me? Was I the exception and not the norm? Right in the midst of our campus and surrounding downtown area were hundreds of homeless people trying to survive each day. What made them any different from me? How had I been able to stumble upon this great opportunity and they hadn't? I saw that there was a very thin line that separated me from others, and that gave me an idea.

TALKING TO MIAMI DADE STUDENTS ABOUT WHAT WAS REALLY GOING ON IN THE LIVES of people less fortunate than us felt like a good start. But then I wondered, *How can we take this to the next level? How can we get students beyond just being aware of the plight of people less fortunate and actually engage in efforts to address their needs? How to get them to understand that it is not the degrees we attain but rather our commitment to attending to others that can make our communities a better place?*

I approached one of my professors with the idea and said, "Why don't we create a student organization at Miami Dade whose primary focus is community service?" Professor Medina readily recognized the value of what I was trying to do. I think part of the reason she came on board so quickly was that she had advocacy blood flowing through her veins, and the other part was because she had an incredible life story that was filled with many triumphs over adversity. Working together, we were able to come up with an organization called the Society of Law and Community Service. I was the inaugural president of the organization, and it's still going on today. It has grown from when I first started it, and it is doing amazing work.

One legacy that I left at the Society of Law and Community Service was our annual toy drive. We partnered with the state attorney's office for Miami-Dade County, the Eleventh Judicial Circuit. We collected toys all over campus and then took them to places where kids were not going to have a good Christmas. Each year we would pick one or two facilities; one time, it actually fell to me to dress up as Santa Claus and hand out the gifts. I'll never forget that day at the Belafonte TACOLCY Center, impacting the lives of children, most of whom were from single-parent households, and seeing the joy in those kids' eyes. Knowing I'd made a difference in someone's life and that, at the same time, I was helping change the perspective of some of the students I shared a college with was powerful. Add to that the fact that I was working with the same state attorney's office that had prosecuted me, that I was now in partnership with them doing something good for the community—that was almost overwhelming.

WANTING TO GROW THE MEMBERSHIP OF THE SOCIETY OF LAW AND COMMUNITY SERVICE, I went around to the different classes on campus and shared my story with folks. I talked to them about the importance of giving back and how fulfilling it was. Through those discussions, students wanted to be a part of it and volunteered. I became almost like a disciple of community service. I was sold on it, and I could convince others to participate because it flowed so naturally from who I was.

Every good thing that's happened to me has happened because I committed to community service and to giving back—not because I wanted it to happen or I asked for it to happen or I prayed for it to happen. I didn't pray for the traditional form of success. I just prayed to do God's work.

Service is my lottery ticket. I told the students, "If you want to hit it big, serving your community is what is guaranteed to win. It's much better than trying to garner some kind of prize that comes from outside of yourself." After all those years of wondering who I was, and what my purpose in life was, when I stumbled onto my purpose, I embraced it and didn't want to let it go. Now, every day I woke up, I had something to engage with, so I knew that whenever I died, I would have made an impact on this planet in some form or fashion. People's lives have been altered either because they heard my story of recovery or we met each other and I did something to help them along the way, whether it was minor or major. These people might not fill up a stadium at my funeral, but what they were doing in response to a little help from me and people like me was so much more important.

Not every student easily bought into the idea of community service being a moral duty to our fellow human beings. I wasn't dismayed by this; I understood that everyone had their own personal experiences and perspectives on engaging or not engaging in community service. For those who didn't get the moral appeal, I spoke to their own educational self-interest. I recounted the opening scene in the movie *21*, in which the main character is a smart student who is applying to medical school. He is sitting in the office of the dean, and the dean is describing the thousands of students who had applied to attend the same medical school, all with the same grades and letters of recommendation from all the right people. After noting how tough the competition is to get into medical school, the dean asks the young man, "Where is your bling?" What the dean wanted to know was what this young man had done that would distinguish him from all the other applicants fighting for the few coveted seats. That distinction, I would tell the students, can come from engaging in community service.

Whether it was education, recovery, or advocacy, it all led back to the same question for me: What am I doing to make our society better? And I was not alone at Miami Dade. It was a special time and place, and we didn't even realize it.

I was among a group of students who were selected by the university to go to Tallahassee to lobby at the state capitol on behalf of the college. There was some legislation that would have freed up some funds so Miami Dade could expand its programs and maintain affordability for people coming in. The group was made up of student leaders from various parts of the university. We were chosen because we had all been active and had participated in student government in some form. We just stood out.

On the bus were a group of Latinx kids I got to know: Felipe Matos, Gaby Pacheco, Juan Rodriguez, and Carlos Roa—you probably recognize those names by now. They were talking about how they were going to walk from Dade County all the way to the White House to deliver a letter to President Barack Obama to ask him to change immigration policy. That was the start of the movement for Deferred Action for Childhood Arrivals (DACA), which allows some rights to individuals, known as "Dreamers," who were brought to the US as children outside of established immigration channels. These four would later organize in 2010 the Trail of Dreams, a 1,500-mile walk from Miami to Washington, DC, to support the passing of the DREAM Act, proposed federal legislation that would provide conditional resident status to undocumented immigrant students of good moral character.

In retrospect, it's pretty amazing that we would all come out of the same place. We didn't realize at that time, of course, that the five of us would go on to impact the lives of millions of people. I'm not sure what it was in that environment that helped us believe we could create change on a large scale. At that moment, though, we were just people who were experiencing some type of pain. It was a shared pain of not belonging to society, not feeling a part of it. Undocumented folks had to pay crazy fees just to go to school and lived constantly under the threat of deportation. Carlos and I sat together, and he told me about how, between work and where he was forced to live to escape detection, he had to get up at three o'clock in the morning to catch the bus to school. He was functioning on very little sleep but had dreams of being an architect. He is one now.

I knew what it felt like to believe I was unwelcome in this country. I didn't feel like I was a part of society because of my criminal history and having my core rights taken away: to serve on a jury, to run for office, to own a firearm, and—most fundamentally—to vote. I felt ostracized because of my previous drug abuse. I was appreciative of the opportunities that I was getting—we all were—but at the same time, it was not enough. Change would have to come.

# EIGHT

# ADVOCACY ON ANOTHER LEVEL

**M**Y INVOLVEMENT WITH the Homeless/Formerly Homeless Forum led me next to walk down two related paths. It was through them that I ended up becoming a board member of the Miami-Dade County Homeless Trust, and through them that I was introduced to the Florida Rights Restoration Coalition. I will always remember the H/FHF as the first organization I made a conscious commitment to be engaged in and where I advocated for something. I was able to work with other directly impacted people and know that the work that we were doing was actually making a difference. It wasn't just about us sharing our stories. It was about us being able to give input to help create policies or even to direct policies and to make decisions as to the strategies involving reducing the homeless population. This advocacy on another level created a thirst in me and others in the group to want to do more.

THE MIAMI-DADE COUNTY HOMELESS TRUST WAS A GOVERNING BODY THAT HELPED facilitate ending homelessness in our county. I first came in contact with them because they were one of two partners, along with the Homeless/Formerly Homeless Forum, that coordinated a yearly candlelight vigil to honor homeless individuals who had passed away. It was celebrated on National Homeless Persons' Memorial Day and held by the fountain near the Stephen P. Clark Center in downtown Miami. We would call out the name of every homeless person who had died during the previous year; there could be as many as a hundred names being read out, one at a time, to raise awareness that there was still an invisible population out there. Some of those people died a natural death, some died a violent death because of crime and because they were easy marks for predators. Some of them were former veterans; some of them were teenagers, while some of them were old enough to be grandparents. There was a story behind each one of those names, and we brought it out in public.

The Homeless/Formerly Homeless Forum had two seats at the table for the Homeless Trust, and they selected me to take up one of those. That was an empowering step on my journey, to be sure. To be able to sit, not only in a room but at the same table, with commissioners of governmental agencies and leading organizations like the United Way and Chapman Partnership, with one of the most powerful lobbyists in Florida as the chair, was pretty mind-blowing. Here I was, a man who, not too long before, had been homeless and in drug treatment, in the same boardroom as these powerful and influential people making decisions that are impacting peoples' lives. That really built up my self-worth.

We met on a monthly basis to administer a homeless reduction program. One of the things I learned while serving on the Homeless Trust board was that homelessness could be defined quite broadly. If you're sleeping on the streets, yes, you're homeless; if you're sleeping in a car, you're homeless. But you're also considered homeless if maybe a family member has given you a bed in a room or you are crashing on someone's couch. Because if that person decides to withdraw their generosity for any reason, then you don't necessarily have a place to go. You may not think of yourself as homeless, but until you have your name on a lease and you're paying rent, then you don't have a home—your home—that's how you're considered.

By that definition, I was homeless for approximately eleven years. The overwhelming majority of that time I was living on the street or squatting in abandoned buildings. But even when I was fortunate enough to be camping out with someone for a time, I couldn't tell you, "I own that home," or, "I'm paying the rent." That was the goal of the Homeless Trust, to get as many people as they could in the state of Florida to be able to say that.

**THE SECOND PATH THAT MY WORK WITH THE HOMELESS/FORMERLY HOMELESS FORUM**
led me to was even more impactful. The forum was a member of the
Florida Rights Restoration Coalition. In 2006, I was able to go on a
trip with fellow members of H/FHF to the annual convening for the
Florida Rights Restoration Coalition in Tampa, Florida, at the Stetson
University College of Law.

Up until that point, I knew very little about the restoration of civil
rights. It wasn't until I attended that convening that I started getting
an understanding of the impact that my felony convictions have had
on my life as they relate to voting, serving on a jury, running for office,
housing, employment, and even something as simple as obtaining a
business license. That convening was the first time I heard the word
"disenfranchisement" in connection to people who were in my situation. We listened to experts from around the state and from around
the country, and I spoke with them personally, including the keynote
speaker, Walter McNeil, who was the secretary for the Florida Department of Corrections.

It was an odd experience. On the one hand, all I had were questions. I wanted to be able to understand everything that was being
discussed, and I was a rookie. My mom always used to tell me that
it's better to be quiet and let people think you're stupid than to open
your mouth and confirm it. In this group of folks who were very
well-versed in felon disenfranchisement, I didn't know what I had to
contribute that was meaningful. At the same time, I grasped that for
some of the folks I was talking with, the discussion was more theoretical. They hadn't experienced the roadblocks and the stigma and the
shame and the frustration. It occurred to me that if I listened well, I
could build the policy knowledge I was lacking and add to their discussion from my bank of personal experiences in a way that could be
very useful for that coalition. I wanted some day for them to be able
to use me as a voice, as I worked my way back up from the bottom.

At that time, the Florida Rights Restoration Coalition (FRRC)
was just as its name states, a coalition of organizations throughout
the state and the country. It included state offices, like the public defender's and state attorney's offices; religious organizations, like the

Episcopal and AME Churches; and civic and nonprofit groups, like the League of Women Voters, the ACLU, the NAACP, the Advancement Project, the Sentencing Project, and the Brennan Center for Justice. It also included smaller grassroots organizations like Brothers of the Same Mind. At one point, there were over seventy independent organizations in the FRRC. All of these organizations came together with a primary focus on the restoration of civil rights for people formerly convicted of felonies.

FRRC wasn't an entity on its own. It was a project housed within the ACLU headquarters in Miami. After the convening, I started attending their steering committee meetings. I learned a lot from the ACLU staffers, who were always around the office, as well as from a gentleman by the name of Elton Edwards. Elton was a highly intelligent man, very professional and knowledgeable, but he had been to prison, and he had gotten a taste of how that would change his life forever. From him, I learned strategies for coordinating all the different individuals from all the different organizations that the coalition had to pull together. Most importantly, I learned that returning citizens have more than their "voice" to contribute in advocacy.

IN THOSE YEARS, FRRC HAD A TWO-FOLD STRATEGY TO CONVINCE POLICYMAKERS ABOUT the importance of felon re-enfranchisement. The first part was to lobby the Florida legislature to make the changes we wanted to see. That effort was not that successful, but we did make some headway on our second front, which was to try to reach the governor and members of his cabinet, which included the attorney general, the chief financial officer, and the commissioner of agriculture. In April 2007, the governor of Florida, Charlie Crist, established new rules that would automatically restore rights for returning citizens so long as they had completed their probation, had no pending criminal charges, and had paid their restitution. Returning citizens with less serious convictions would have their rights restored automatically, while returning citizens with more serious convictions would have to apply to have their rights restored.

It sounded amazing, except the term "automatically" was pretty misleading. The restoration of voting rights was automatic more in name than in nature. The only people who really felt the immediate benefits of that policy were those who were incarcerated at the time it was put into effect. For those folks, approximately six months before they completed their sentence, the department of corrections would send their paperwork to the Florida parole commission to be processed. By the time those individuals had completed their sentences and were walking out of their prison cells, they would get a certificate saying that their rights had been restored. For those who were not incarcerated, however, even if they had been convicted of less serious offenses, they still had to apply for the restoration of their rights just like the returning citizens with more serious convictions did. That created a huge backlog of people submitting their applications to be processed, because that population consisted of approximately 1.54 million people who had completed their sentence at the time, and many of them wanted to get their rights back.

The other reason for the backlog was that at the same time the new policies were implemented, the agency that was tasked with processing these applications, the Florida parole commission, had its budget slashed dramatically. Where at one point they may have had, say, fifteen people working on processing applications, that number was reduced to five. So you had a smaller staff and a huge influx of applications coming in at the same time, which created a massive bottleneck. At one point there were over one hundred thousand people waiting for their rights to be restored.

Nonetheless, the policy was a major victory. FRRC put on workshops throughout the state of Florida, which I attended. These events, which occurred at various spots around the state simultaneously, helped people apply for the restoration of their civil rights. During a four-year period, over 155,000 people were able to get their rights back, and the FRRC played a significant role in helping that happen.

WHEN THE FOLKS AT FRRC SAW HOW ENTHUSED I WAS AT THE CONVENING, THEY nominated me to become the steering committee secretary. I was already doing so much in my life: running the three-quarter-way house and going to meetings, supporting my own sobriety as well as other peoples', and then being in school and mentoring others through the

Law Center, and running the Society of Law and Community Service. . . . But there was no way I could say no. They nominated me, and I didn't shy away from it.

Being secretary meant that I had to be on monthly conference calls with all of these experts. My job was to transcribe the call and prepare meeting minutes for the next call. Now, I was no typist, but in the end it worked out to my advantage, because while everyone else on that call got one hour of education, I ended up getting eight hours of education—that was how long it would take me to type up the transcript between listening and fast forwarding and rewinding over and over again to make sure I heard things correctly and got them down properly.

All of that knowledge and the strategies and the different points about felon disenfranchisement—I was getting it eight times more than everybody else. This went on every single month for about three or four years. Sometimes things would be mentioned that would send me off doing research, because I definitely wanted to be able to understand everything that was being discussed. Little did I know at the time that I was being set up to be in the position that I am in today. When our president resigned, the committee looked around and saw I was the most active directly impacted person in the organization at the time. As a body, FRRC had previously determined that it wanted to move impacted people to the forefront, to have them be more involved in the processes and the decision-making and the strategies. So here I was, I'd been on the calls for years now. I knew all the key players. I knew all the key organizations. I got along well with people. It was just natural for them to ask me to be the interim president until the next convening was held. I was subsequently voted in as the president. The "interim" was taken off my title in 2010, and I've been the president ever since.

NOT TOO LONG AFTER I WAS VOTED IN AS PRESIDENT OF FRRC, WE HAD A NEW GOVERNOR take office in Florida. His name was Rick Scott, and he was a former executive at a healthcare company. Charlie Crist had chosen not to run for a second term, so the election came down to Scott versus the Democratic candidate, Alex Sink. Sink had been the state's chief financial officer, and she was the first woman elected to the state cabinet in more than a decade. The election was close—it was decided by 1 percentage point—fewer than sixty thousand votes. There was a bit of a red wave that came over Florida at the time, and Rick Scott benefited from the Tea Party's rise to prominence, as well as running in opposition to the Affordable Care Act.

One of the first things that Governor Scott did was to roll back the clemency policies for the restoration of rights to returning citizens. I was baffled. Neither Scott nor his attorney general, Pam Bondi, had run on a platform addressing the restoration of civil rights. Neither of them mentioned rights restoration prominently in their campaigns, and I'd never heard them make any statements or take any positions either for or against it, in fact. Yet that was their very first official act as a Cabinet once in office.

They rolled back the previous policies and made it even more difficult for people to actually get their rights restored. Now people had to wait either five or seven years before they were even allowed to apply, based on the level of the severity of the crime. This waiting period even affected people in the backlog. They weren't grandfathered in. It wasn't as if an application was already submitted; they would still fall under the old policy.

I was one of those people in the backlog. I had submitted my application in 2006. Now, in 2011, five years later, I finally got a letter saying that I didn't even qualify to apply because I'd had to wait seven years owing to the nature of my crime. So my application had been rejected. A bunch of us from FRRC went to Tallahassee to try to lobby the governor. There were a lot of grassroots organizations, along with organizations affiliated with the FRRC, that mobilized to go before the clemency board. Mark Schlakman, a professor out of Florida State University, testified and said basically that this went against common sense. Making it more difficult for people to reintegrate back into their community was counterproductive. It goes against what studies have clearly shown: the quicker we help a person reintegrate into their community, the less likely they are to re-offend.

I remember one moment hearing from the commissioner of agriculture, Adam Putnam, who asked if there was any empirical data that supported changing the policy, to make it more difficult for people with felony convictions to be re-enfranchised. Of course, there was no answer to his question because there weren't any studies that justified Scott's new policy. But we knew that one member of the clemency board at least had some misgivings, even though he still didn't vote against it, in spite of all the testimony. It passed unanimously and was a very depressing moment that took the wind right out of our sails.

We spent so much time and money and energy and resources to get to the policy that Governor Crist had implemented. It wasn't a perfect solution in 2007, but we were able to help a lot of people. To see all that work evaporate, to be for naught, devastated a lot of people. A lot of organizations were frustrated. It dampened a lot of spirits. There wasn't that much energy around FRRC after that. A lot of folks fell off because they didn't see what else we could possibly do.

Here I was, the newly elected president, and we were dealt this crushing blow. I didn't have any hatred in my heart, but I was sorely disappointed. To have all of our work undone by just the signature on a piece of paper? Just like none of that work mattered? I couldn't get over it. I kept thinking, *Wow, you mean to tell me that four politicians have that much power, where they can decide which American citizen gets to vote and which American citizens don't get to vote? They can have that decision become a policy or a law with just the stroke of a pen?* That was way too much power for any politician to have. Whether you were a Democrat or a Republican, it didn't matter. To see politicians trivialize civil rights, and to see how partisan politics played a role in that, was heartbreaking.

It was our lowest point as an organization, but it was also the beginning of the way back up to great heights. That moment marked the beginning of a new FRRC, and it truly set the stage for Amendment 4.

# NINE

# DAVID AND GOLIATH

THEY SAY WHEN LIFE throws lemons at you, you catch them and make lemonade. When the level of enthusiasm and support for felon re-enfranchisement died down after Governor Scott's crushing blow, I looked at it as an opportunity to fulfill the original intent of FRRC, which had been verbalized back in 2006. At that time, we said we wanted more directly impacted people involved. As the primary focus of the big-name organizations moved elsewhere, it allowed me the space to reshape the Florida Rights Restoration Coalition. I had to find a way to rally the troops and get them engaged.

I decided to take the same approach with felon re-enfranchisement that I would with any other issues that might impact me. I'm not going to wait for somebody else to try to figure out and tell me what the solution is. I'm not going to wait for anybody else to take up the fight. If it means that much to me, then I have to be the initiator, because if I rely on somebody else, they're not going to have that same level of energy or commitment.

When I first joined FRRC it was housed within the Florida ACLU's headquarters, in Miami. Most people thought of our project as coming out of the ACLU's office. That was problematic in a couple of ways. It made it difficult for us to get into certain doors, when people heard FRRC and thought ACLU. There is sometimes a tense relationship between the ACLU and law enforcement, and we needed to get law enforcement more engaged in our conversations if we were going to move our agenda forward. There is sometimes a tense relationship between the ACLU and minority communities, as there often is between well-funded national organizations and grassroots organizations with a different perspective of what's happening on the ground.

While we appreciated the support and the work of the ACLU, it was time to become a stand-alone organization led by directly affected people. We needed to shift from being basically part of other organizations to an organization that mainly comprised impacted individuals. We began thinking this around the time that the ACLU's funding for the project dried up, so we were basically on our own anyway. For a while, the ACLU let us use their offices and their phones, but eventually the money for that ran out as well. We didn't have any money. We didn't have any donors. We didn't have anybody on payroll. We lost our website.

There was no support out there for FRRC. For a time, the FRRC office was my car. I worked out of there or out of the recovery house. It was just me and some dedicated folks throughout the state who still wanted to do the work. We were like a boat without an engine. We had the rudder, the direction of where we wanted to head, but we didn't have the power to get where we wanted to go.

When we entered that valley, when folks dropped off, strangely I was not afraid. Plenty of people said that if these big-name organizations fall off, if so-and-so leaves, this thing is over with. But I never believed that. From my upbringing in the Christian faith, I was easily reminded how God used the least among a group of people to bring about the greatest change. The story of David and Goliath illustrated that perfectly.

I remember thinking about that story while I was in prison. It made sense to me that God would have things unfold that way to show his power. If he used a strong guy to beat up somebody weaker, that wouldn't show how good he is. The miracle comes, or the belief comes, when he chooses someone who seemingly should not even have a chance against another person, but, through God's power, this seemingly weaker person overcomes the obstacles. I saw that on the inside: Nobody got any credit for beating up somebody who was weaker than them. As a matter of fact, we would probably look down on the big guy, right? Because he needed to pick on somebody his own size. God was not the Goliath God. He was the God of David. That spiritual concept reinforced to me that this fight to restore civil rights to returning citizens was a spiritual effort. When a major organization withdrew its support, I thought to myself, *This falls right in line with how God operates.* Little did I know that this experience would not be the last time organizations walked away from FRRC or the effort.

In Matthew 25, Jesus says it this way: "I tell you that whenever you refused to do it for the least important of these people, you refused to do it for me." We were the least among us. God always uses the least among a group of people to bring about the biggest change. And even for those in the fight who didn't have a religious orientation or even any belief in God at all, these truths held, and they have a powerful message.

ONE OF THE FIRST THINGS THAT I WANTED TO DO WITH THE RECREATED FRRC WAS A statewide day of action. It would be called the "Right Now" rally to signify that we wanted our rights right now, not seven years later or five years later. We would hold rallies on Human Rights Day in Tampa, Orlando, Jacksonville, Tallahassee, and throughout Broward County simultaneously, publicly demanding that we have our rights restored.

In the process of planning these rallies, we came to find out something very interesting. In Tampa, for example, our point person found a great location. We were in the process of securing the space, and the owners of the facilities asked us for our nonprofit paperwork in order for them to give us the space free of charge. "What paperwork is that?" I asked. "You know, your 501(c)(3) documents that show you have been approved by the IRS as a tax-exempt, charitable organization." I went looking for them, but I couldn't find them. I asked around, and that's when I discovered that FRRC was not an official entity in the state of Florida. It's like we didn't even exist. That was a perfect metaphor for the way someone with a felony conviction is made to feel.

At that moment I decided, *Let's make this organization official.* In 2011, we became Florida Rights Restoration Coalition, Inc. In order to file the necessary paperwork, I had to have a board. Who better to have on this board than returning citizens? I connected with Jessica

Chiappone (now Younts), a returning citizen who had gone on to law school and eventually passed the New York Bar Exam and who had presented her testimony about returning-citizen disenfranchisement practices in Florida to the UN in Switzerland. She became our vice president. Our secretary was Dr. Rosalind Osgood, who was also a returning citizen. She is now a school-board member in Broward County, with an amazing story of redemption, including getting both her master's and doctoral degrees, despite innumerable obstacles thrown in her way.

Dr. Osgood was the only one who'd had her rights restored at the time we created our board, but we all had some powerful stories, and when we got together some magic would happen. One of the challenges we were trying to address was how we should refer to ourselves and the people we were working for. There was a study that had come out of Florida State University, which had one of the leading doctoral programs in criminology, a few years earlier, published in an article as "The Labeling of Convicted Felons and Its Consequences for Recidivism." It basically said that the receipt of a felony label could increase the likelihood of recidivism; calling someone an ex-offender, an ex-con, or an ex-felon makes them more likely to return to a life of crime.

The study reminded me of how we used to always hear that if you keep calling children stupid, they're going to grow up thinking that they're stupid. Let's not lead with the fact that someone was formerly convicted of a crime. Let's lead with their humanity. We wanted people to see us as human beings first, not as an ex-anything. The word we landed on was "citizen." Then we added "returning," because we were citizens who had made mistakes, had been incarcerated, and had done our time, and now we were returning to our community.

We were returning citizens. That was a powerful descriptor, and we intended to take advantage of that power.

AFTER THE RIGHT NOW RALLIES, ROSALIND, JESSICA, AND I HEADED OFF ACROSS THE state talking to people about the plight of returning citizens. We just wanted to keep Floridians aware of the destructive policies that were affecting people like us, and to believe that this was a relevant issue in addition to the other issues these people might be focusing on at the time. Don't forget about us, was the core of the message. We appreciate you as old partners and allies, and we're not trying to grab your exclusive focus. But felon disenfranchisement is a legitimate issue that deserves to be on folks' radars.

When opportunities came up to speak on the issue, I would call Jessica or Rosalind, and one of us would go. There weren't many speaking engagements initially available to us, but we found them where we could. It could be at a rally or a march, and we would claim a few minutes for our issue. We might be speaking to a group of professionals, sharing our stories and trying to connect with individuals one-on-one. We might go to an NAACP meeting or a community neighborhood association meeting. If we couldn't get ourselves invited, we would show up there anyway; even if it was just to have a conversation with an organization leader, we took that opportunity. We started getting a grant here and a donation there. Slowly but surely, one person at a time, we were bringing people back in.

THE OTHER PART OF GOING AROUND THE STATE OF FLORIDA WAS TO MEET WITH RETURNING citizens. We knew they were going to be the new lifeblood of our movement. Whenever we found out what other returning citizens were doing locally, we would go to support it. I would take money from my student loans and travel tens of thousands of miles around the state. I put over fifty thousand miles on my car in one year alone working on this campaign and never leaving the state of Florida, just talking to people in order to establish relationships with them. If you had asked me where we were located, I couldn't give you an address. If you asked me for an office phone number, I couldn't give you one. But I could talk about the organization and the vision that we had to one day be a force in the state of Florida to accurately reflect the voices of directly impacted people.

I didn't have great expectations that everybody who heard about us was going to embrace what we were trying to do. We were just trying to keep it moving. My philosophy was that if you told a hundred people, maybe five or ten would rock with you, so I just kept talking to as many people as possible. Eventually, in almost every major city, there would be people who just stood out. They believed in what we were talking about, even though they hadn't seen the advanced plans yet. People like Michael Orlando or Devin Coleman in Jacksonville, who both eventually became board members for FRRC, as did the Reverend Greg James in Tallahassee. These little pinpoints of light came from people of all economic statuses; they were Black, Brown, and white; they were men and women, and I maintained close relationships with those folks.

MY JOB AS I UNDERSTOOD IT WAS TO MAKE SURE THAT THE PLIGHT OF RETURNING CITIZENS was still at least in people's peripheral vision. No matter what some other group was working on—from an immigration advocacy organization to the Sierra Club's concern for the environment—I would talk to them about how FRRC impacted their cause. I would tailor my argument. I didn't want to be obnoxious about it, but every opportunity I had, I would insert a discussion of felon disenfranchisement.

Someone could be talking about educational disparities, and I would be able to say, "Well, do you know that more money is spent on incarceration than is spent on education?" If an organization was trying to reduce gun violence, I'd say, "Well, restoring a person's civil rights and finding other means for that person to be successful is a means of reducing the number of people in our community that have guns and that might use them for bad reasons." I pointed out that labor organizations and economic justice champions alike would benefit if we reduced the recidivism rate. And the way to do that was to help a person reintegrate into their community, and one of the ways you help them reintegrate and have a stake in the community is by restoring their civil rights.

To everyone I met, I said some version of this: "If we're able to solve this, it'll make your work easier." When you have over a million people who are barred from participating in elections, that's a million people you lose who could have helped influence or elect policymakers, who care about your cause. I was very assertive, and I think that all of that assertiveness helped create somewhat of a buzz.

Of course, there were some people who listened, and some people who didn't. We were making a bit of progress, but there were some stiff headwinds. That was the year that a lot of cities in the state of Florida did not have enough money in their budget and were forcing the police and firefighters' unions back to the table to renegotiate collective bargaining agreements. There were threats of laying off firefighters and police officers, and that was consuming a lot of civic attention. The legislature was trying to pass one bill to privatize prisons in Florida and another that would allow juvenile offenders to be housed in adult facilities. Both of those initiatives would only increase inequities in the basic functioning of the criminal justice system, and resources and energy needed to be put into fighting them.

I UNDERSTOOD ALL OF THAT. I COULD BE PATIENT. MY FAITH WAS STRONG THAT EVERY time there was a challenge ahead, a way would be made. If anything, these years caused my concept of faith to mature. I had heard that faith was "the substance of things hoped for, the evidence of things not seen." Now my faith had grown to the point where I expected God to show up when he was supposed to. I didn't worry about how or when things were going to get done. From what direction was he going to come? I didn't need to know on a rational level. I only had to have confidence in my expectations.

# TEN

# A BALLOT INITIATIVE?

THE FURTHER I DOVE into felon disenfranchisement, its history and its impact, the more powerful the flame grew inside me to see justice restored. I was constantly interacting with people who were impacted by these policies, whether they were returning citizens coming to the recovery house that I was managing on a daily basis or people I was coming into contact with as I traveled around the state trying to pull together FRRC as an organization. So many of these people were good people who happened to live in a state with repressive laws.

Whenever I thought about how an elected official was able to control life for so many people with just a signature on a paper, it sat heavy in my heart. By 2011, there were an estimated 1.4 million Floridians who couldn't vote because of a felony conviction (that still included me), and we couldn't figure out the right way to help them. One way was to petition the governor and his cabinet, including the clemency board, but that had worked against us. We weren't totally satisfied with the policy that Charlie Crist had implemented, but it was something, and it had allowed over 155,000 people to register to vote. To see that those rights hung at the mercy of whoever occupied the governor's mansion next and whatever he or she might be feeling was untenable.

Another way to try to accomplish our goals was to work with the state legislature. Trying to get a bunch of politicians to agree on something is daunting, and at one point we worked with a lobbyist to help us understand the way power flowed around the halls of the capitol. It was so complex. In order to even get something to the floor for a vote, it had to get out of various committees. You could do a lot of work, and get real movement on a bill, only to have it die in one committee. It could be the last committee to hear the bill, and it could just languish there because the chair of that committee didn't put it on the agenda. And if the bill is not on the agenda, it can't be heard. Once again, it was power concentrated in the hands of a few people who for whatever reason didn't care to support returning citizen re-enfranchisement.

The final way to restore our rights was a ballot initiative. To pass a ballot initiative you need 60 percent of the vote and not just a simple majority. But still, there were at least 1.4 million people affected by these policies. I was sure that we could find enough directly impacted people, returning citizens, to get five to ten members of their families or their networks to pledge to vote for the restoration of their rights. What would it be like if only half of those people were able to get family members and friends out to vote on their behalf?

Right from the beginning, though, we met opposition. Lots of people told us why we would not be successful. It was too expensive to run a ballot initiative, they said. There was very low public support for the issue. It had been tried, but no real headway had been made, so it had been abandoned after only a few petitions were signed. *Slow down*, I felt like saying. *Talk to me about these issues one at a time.*

In that, I took my cue from President Obama, who was rounding out his first term at the time. When he first announced that he was running for the highest office in the land, nobody knew who Barack Obama was. People told him he didn't have a chance. Obama didn't spend all his time with the people who already supported him. He went to the people who said he wasn't qualified and asked them, "Well, why don't you think I can be president?" Whatever reply they came back with, he came back with his own reply, and a conversation was started. It was through this engagement that he was able to start winning people over slowly, all the way to the point where he got to the Democratic National Convention because a majority of Democrats had said that, yes, he can be the president. He has what it takes.

After Obama got the nomination, then he had to go against his Republican counterpart. More people who questioned his level of experience came out of the woodwork. They ran ads asking America, "Is that who you want, when that call comes at midnight? Is this who you want answering?" Obama continued, however, to not just play to his base. He went to people who did not believe that he could be the commander in chief, and he talked to them. Slowly, but surely, he was able to convince people, or at least have them cast doubt on their own firmly held notions. And in the end, he had more people saying that he could be president than people saying that he couldn't.

In a similar way, when I heard people telling me what couldn't be done, that just made me work even harder. When people told me something was not going to work, I asked them to explain to me why it wasn't going to work. I took in their explanation and used it to help shape my thinking. I was always seeking ways to improve our strategy because, *Who am I? I've never run a ballot initiative before or done anything like that. I'm just a formerly homeless drug addict from Miami. What do I know about running a statewide operation or the politics involved and all of that?* I don't know what I don't know.

There were some folks who were just naysayers, and I couldn't get very far with them. But then you had some folks who were not just naysayers. They were willing to engage in a conversation and be converted. So those were the individuals who I consistently went back to. If you're willing to show me what you believe is the right way or to explain to me why you think my way is wrong, then I can work with you, because you're teaching me something. I would actually thank you for destroying some of my thinking. That would force me to go back to the drawing board and be better prepared, so that when I came to you, you were not going to destroy the same thing. Maybe you'd find something else, but now I knew that first thing was solid.

I was especially open to constructive criticism when I could see that my adversary was saying no because I hadn't presented the issue to them in the right way, at least not yet. They weren't saying no because they didn't think it was the right thing to do or because they didn't believe in the value of returning citizens as human beings. They were just saying no to what I'd presented to them. So, I needed to tighten up my presentation. As I tightened things up, little by little, I'd find a person here and a person there who said you might be onto something.

I did extensive canvassing to unearth all the objections to a ballot initiative to re-enfranchise felons. The most powerful one turned out to be the result of a grisly event that had made national headlines and resulted in sweeping changes in legislation just a few years prior.

Jessica Marie Lunsford was a nine-year-old girl from southwest Florida who had been abducted and murdered. She was taken from her home by a registered sex offender who lived nearby; the details, including the rape and means of death, were beyond heartbreaking. In response, Florida created the Jessica Lunsford Act, which tightened controls on sexual offenders registering within the counties they lived in, such as having them wear electronic tracking devices or even increasing their initial prison sentences. Before long, forty-two states had implemented some form of "Jessica's Law."

Around that time, a Quinnipiac poll was taken that showed very low support from Florida voters for the restoration of rights for returning citizens. It seemed that a wide variety of respondents conflated the meaning of "ex-offender" and "sex offender." The two groups were so thoroughly associated that any further discussion would have to clearly redefine the terms in people's minds. This was where I thought that switching the focus to the term "returning citizens" would prove to be most useful.

DURING THIS TIME, WE TRIED A LOT OF WAYS TO MAKE FIGHTING FELON DISENFRANchisement a more popular issue. FRRC was due to have our next convening, and I wanted to find a keynote speaker who would attract people and make them want to get in that room. A very popular speaker of the day was Professor Charles Ogletree from Harvard. He had a new book coming out that year, *Life Without Parole: America's New Death Penalty?*, which he coedited, so I knew we were on the same page as far as the potential overreach of the criminal justice system.

I found out that Professor Ogletree was going to be in Tallahassee around the time of the convening, giving a presentation at the annual gathering of the Florida Legislative Black Caucus. I drove up with a friend to see if we could meet with him. I didn't have a team of folks to help me snag some A-list personality to speak, and I definitely didn't have the money to pay for anyone. I just felt if I could get next to Ogletree, I could convince him to be the keynote speaker at our convening.

We ended up missing the event, or rather his speaking portion, but there were still some people milling around. I ran into a lady who had heard me speak at a community center several weeks before. She ran up to me and said, "I got somebody for you to meet!" She introduced me to a lady by the name of Salandra. As it turns out, Salandra was standing right next to her sister, Sheena. I was introduced to both of them. After being introduced, I looked at Sheena and said, "I think I'm supposed to meet you."

Sheena thought it was a pick-up line, of course. I don't blame her. But I was not like that. I was still in the business of protecting my sobriety. I just felt overwhelmed when I was in her presence. Sheena and Salandra were there as part of a group called the Black Women's Roundtable. They were going back to their hotel, which was up a hill. I found myself trudging along after them, and I'm telling you, that was a steep hill. I was out of breath by the time we were halfway (my days of being in top form and playing football were long behind me), but I was determined to get to that hotel. When I got there, I ended up having the opportunity to share my story with Sheena and tell her what I was trying to do.

The same day, we had lunch, and then she left to drive back down to Central Florida. I remember talking to her on the phone her entire way there, telling her I wanted to meet her mom. The funny thing was, I had met her mom a few months before. I was speaking at an event, and her mom was waiting in a line of people who wanted to talk to me afterward. She introduced herself and then went back and told her family about this amazing young man she had met.

When I made the connection with Sheena, I knew that this was the woman I was supposed to be with. I didn't want to come off as too aggressive, but I was very confident that this woman was supposed to be in my life. The next day, I drove back from Tallahassee to Miami, and then I turned right around to drive back up to Central Florida because I wanted to have dinner with Sheena on Valentine's Day. On our date, I told her that she was the one. I know that she was a little thrown off because she had been having people describe the man she was going to meet, and I checked all of the boxes. Everything just fit right into place.

Sheena's birthday was in June. She had heard me sing before, a line or two during our courting phase, so when she invited me to her birthday party, she asked me to perform there. I told her, "No, I won't sing." She kept asking me, and I kept turning her down because I had decided that I was going to sing as part of proposing to her. She had no clue.

For the birthday party, her dad came down from Philadelphia, so both her parents were at the party. I took them aside and asked their permission to propose to their daughter. They gave it to me. I then approached Sheena in the middle of the dance floor and started to sing the song "One in a Million You" by Larry Graham. By the time that night had arrived, she knew I was going to sing, but she didn't know that I was going to propose. Near the end of the song, I got on my knees and produced the ring.

Basically, I told her that I thought God had placed us in each other's lives to do his work. She had such an amazing story, having overcome so much as a teenage mother, dealing with all kinds of obstacles, to be who she was at the time, and I recognized that. I told her, "God uses broken people, people who have gone through traumatic things to have an impact in their community and society." I recognized that bringing the two of us together was just the beginning of something that was going to be beautiful—and not just for us. Our number-one priority has always been our community, our world.

Sheena jumped right in. When we started dating, she told me everything I was doing wrong. She called me "the broke organizer." She told me that she believed in what I was trying to do, but she had all kinds of useful critiques about how I could do it better. I was still using a Yahoo account. She told me about Gmail. She taught me how to use technology to be more organized, to really be able to promote the work I was trying to accomplish. She wrote out a whole mini-campaign plan for me and gave it to me, saying, "If you really want to be impactful, these are the things you have to think about."

We didn't have a building or a website or any staff. Sheena was instrumental in helping to make all of that happen. She was not just the organizing director; she was the communications director, the operations director, and the administrative professional. She was all of that wrapped up in the one. Everything she touched made us who we are today. When people look at FRRC, they often comment that we are ahead of the curve with the quality of our materials. Sheena did that.

What she wanted to be, and became, was director of strategic partnerships and relationships and projects. Something she said that has really stuck to me was that we didn't want to just be in a transactional relationship with our donors. We wanted to be in an authentic relationship, to be able to engage them in such a way that it wasn't just, *Write a check and go about your business.* No, we wanted you to be a part of this journey with us. When that happened, that funder, that donor, had a personal buy-in to the work we were doing, and it really helped stimulate strong support for the organization.

I tell folks that my wife has more organizing skills in her pinky than I do in my entire body, multiple times over. We met in February of 2012. I proposed to her in June of 2012. We got married on 12/12/12, by the woman who baptized me as a baby on the US Virgin Island of Saint Croix. And we have been by each other's side ever since.

# ELEVEN

# LAW SCHOOL

URING THIS TIME, something else happened in my life that I could never have predicted: I went to law school. During college, a professor or two of mine mentioned that they thought I would make a great lawyer. It was a compliment, but I didn't really take it too seriously. As my graduation from college drew near, however, I started looking into it more seriously. I now had my bachelor's degree in public safety management, with a concentration in criminal justice. I could do good work with that degree, but how much more would I be able to do with graduate school on my resume? I saw there were folks who had previous criminal convictions who were lawyers or were taking the bar exams in their state. I didn't know whether the loss of my civil rights in Florida would impede my ability to practice law. What I did understand was that, even if you had a checkered past, you were still able to go to law school. And that that sounded like a thrilling intellectual place.

The drive to go to law school came from the desire to understand as much as I possibly could about the law, in order to be of more service to others. I didn't know if I was going to be a lawyer or not. There were so many hoops you had to jump through. When you graduate from law school with a past like mine, they put you through a fitness review where they pepper you with all types of questions to determine if you have been rehabilitated. Have you risen to a level where you're able to be an attorney? I felt comfortable in my answers, but when the subjective judgment of other people is involved, there's always a possibility that things won't go your way.

I could understand why they would want to grill me. Being an attorney is a very serious profession. People are often at their most vulnerable when they deal with an attorney. Sometimes a lawyer can be entrusted with overseeing a lot of money. You might end up with insider knowledge because your clients are revealing a lot of information to you, and you can't take advantage of that knowledge for your own personal gain or the gain of someone who's close to you. You have to be as honest as the day is long, because as a lawyer you are an officer of the court. A lawyer does not have to place a hand on the Bible, like those who testify in a trial do when they swear that whatever they say is the truth, the whole truth, and nothing but the truth. Once you're sworn into the profession, you are always under oath, in a sense, and the court takes what you say to be the truth.

At times I thought *Well, if I were a lawyer, what would I do?* I would be a solo practitioner who represented people who could not afford me. I wasn't going to law school so I could make the most money. If I did charge a six-figure retainer like some kind of Johnnie Cochran, I would make sure I was worth it. But a few of those clients would allow me to do my real work, which would be to take on people who had been wronged. Clients like the grandson of an old friend growing up: he had just been framed for murder. He couldn't afford a top-flight attorney who was dedicated to him and not juggling dozens of state-assigned cases. I imagined representing him and helping him get treatment to get his life back together. I would keep him from getting caught up in our criminal justice system. That's the type of lawyer I wanted to be.

That was the frame of mind I had when I matriculated at Florida International University College of Law. At the end of the day, I wanted to help people. I wanted to make a difference. That included my fellow classmates. You hear all these horror stories about how competitive law school is, how people tear sections out of law books so nobody else can read them. I told my new colleagues, "Listen, I'm not here to be better than you. I'm here to be the best that I can possibly be. What that means is if there's an opportunity to help you be the best that you can possibly be, that makes me better."

In my own small way, I was out to change the culture and perception of law school. In general, I don't believe we have to tear each other down in order to get ahead in life. I don't believe we have to deny others access in order for us to get ahead. I wasn't going to try to hide something from a classmate; I was going to share what I'd learned. I believed that our greatness comes from helping others become great; our strength comes from empowering the weakest among us. To some degree that went against the environment that you find a lot in law school. For example, every class is graded on a curve. Only so many people can get an A, so many a B, a C, all the way down. I found out that it's not good enough just to be right in law school. You have to be more right than the other person.

I thought this experience might help me with my work on the ballot initiative. That was another area of my life where I had to convince people to see things my way, and not only to convince them but to be the most convincing person they came across. When you have fourteen million voters, it's not good enough just to be saying, "This is the right thing." You had to be able to sell your position better than any opposition could, or better than any widespread misconceptions would.

The first year of law school was similar in many ways to undergraduate school. There were some basic core courses you had to take: Common Law, Legal Writing, Contracts, Civil Procedures, Criminal Law. These are the foundations of everything that follows in your next two years. Going into law school, one of the things that I heard was how you couldn't work during your first year. They discourage you from taking a job because school is so hard and intense. I just couldn't give up the rest of my life though. I had to continue to manage the three-quarter-way house and mentor folks there, because that played such a big role in my sobriety. I had to go on with my advocacy work. Asking me to not do that work was like asking me not to breathe.

That first year of law school is the make-or-break year. That's when most people drop out. My first semester, I didn't do so well in my Contracts class. Maybe I had too many other things going on; I don't know. But they put me on academic probation. They let me know that I could not finish my first year under a certain GPA. That put even more pressure on the second semester, but I had a certain degree of confidence that I was getting the hang of things, and besides, in my second semester, I was going to get to take a class I knew a lot about, unfortunately: Criminal Law.

Of all the classes I took my first year in law school, Criminal Law was the one I really took to. A lot of the things the professor and the readings talked about I had some knowledge of, as I've been arrested multiple times and have also appeared before judges, and I had also helped so many other people in prison with their appeals. Because my real-life experiences made that course not too difficult for me, I took some time to mentor some of my classmates all through the semester and especially when it came time to take the final exam.

One of the things about law school is you don't have any way to measure how well you're doing in a particular class because you only take one exam at the end. You go to lectures throughout the whole semester, and then at the end you sit for a huge, three-hour exam. That's it; whatever you get, you get. You don't know, say, halfway through, if you're weak in one area. There are no hard indicators that you're not getting it, nothing glaring that would give you the opportunity to make adjustments.

At the end of the second semester, we had three weeks to study for our exams. A lot of students in our Criminal Law class separated into study groups to help each other. They would pass around written chronological outlines that covered everything that was discussed in class, from start to finish, with key headers for the different subjects within the course. There are various methods of studying. What I did was to connect with a few folks, and we found a room to lock ourselves in and we would lecture to each other. We went over the material, piece by piece. When it came to be my turn, a lot of it was in my head, so I could just lecture from memory.

We got through the study period and went ahead and took the exam. In law school, when you take an exam, you can feel good about it, but you never know what you're going to actually get for a grade, so there's a lot of anxiety. I remember at the end of my first semester, I kept checking the student portal trying to see how I did. They take so long to post your grades. The professors have to read through each exam, and then compare them all to each other to figure out that dreaded curve, so there's a lot of work for them to do. Meanwhile, you're just going crazy. School is over; you're waiting on your grades. I had promised myself that I was not going to go through that torture again at the end of the second semester. Instead, I was going to get away, leave the country. I decided to go on a vacation back to the Virgin Islands. I had not revisited my birthplace since I left as a little kid. It felt like the perfect place to enjoy myself and block out all this law school stuff.

I did manage to relax and be a tourist while visiting. Midway through my vacation, I got a call from a classmate. He was speaking very excitedly, and our phone connection wasn't that good, but I heard him say, "Oh my God! I just wanted to call and thank you for tutoring me. I ended up getting an A in Crim Law."

When I heard that, I felt good because I'd been able to help out a colleague. This wasn't just fluff on my part. I truly believe that service to others is the best way to do God's will. I also felt good because I figured that if I knew the material well enough to help someone else get a good grade, then that meant I was going to get a good grade in the class as well.

Plus, it was Criminal Law—that's my bread and butter! If I don't know any other subject, I'm going to know Crim Law, because of my experience. Right after that call, I got a call from another guy who said he got a B+. So I started putting things together. *If he got an A . . . and he got a B+ . . . I know at the very worst, I got a C+. If I get a C+, I'm good. That means I survived my academic probation and made it out of year one.*

After that second call, I broke my self-imposed moratorium on checking my grades and went into the online student portal. I was scanning my grades to see what I got in Crim Law, because that was the immediate reason I was there; it was like I couldn't even see the other grades. It was an F. I remember refreshing the screen, going back out and coming back in again. *This has got to be a mistake.* Out of all my classes for the entire year, the one that I was most confident in was Criminal Law. I was confident almost to the point that I may have been a little cocky about it. This was my class. I went back in for the fourth or fifth time and saw there was still an F there.

Was it a mistake? Did law schools make mistakes? My mind was blown. Could this be straightened out? The next thing I did was go into my emails, and I found one there from the school. The email basically told me that I had been dismissed from law school. It was not a mistake. That's when the roof caved in.

All I can remember thinking was, *I am a recovering addict. I am far away from home. There's money in my bank account to get as much dope as I want.* My hotel room was right above a bar. In my room, in fact, were six bottles of Cruzan Rum that I had purchased for my family. I am reading an email telling me I've been kicked out of law school. Thoughts are racing through my mind. *How can I face people? I can't go back to the continental United States. There are so many people who are counting on me, who are proud of me for overcoming so much in my life and getting into law school. There were articles written about me. People were inspired. All of this and it turns out I'm just a fraud. How can I look people in the eye?*

It was the perfect storm, one of only two times that my recovery has been seriously tested, the first one being the Spider-Man Massacre. Luckily, something kicked in. They tell you that whenever you're feeling like you're getting ready to relapse, pick up the phone and call your sponsor. I called Frank at the three-quarter-way house. I had to tell him the situation I was in and how I was feeling. Maybe he could give me some guidance on what to do. I had previously gone to an AA meeting in Saint Croix; for some reason I hadn't been able to find an NA meeting. Maybe Frank would tell me to find the very next AA meeting?

I called him and he picked up. As soon as I said, "What's up, Frank?" he started fussing about a whole bunch of stuff that was happening at the recovery house while I'd been gone. He was telling me about all these different situations with our clients while I was waiting my turn to speak. But that turn never came. With each little vignette Frank shared, I started obsessing about my own situation less. I never got to tell him what was going on. Just hearing his voice and hearing what was going on with the guys took me out of my funk. It really pulled me back from that relapse I was about to have.

One of the things that I discovered during recovery was that speaking up at a meeting was not just for the other people at the treatment center; it was also for you. It might actually be more for you than for the other people there, because it helps you stay grounded. When you're talking, you find yourself saying some things you weren't thinking consciously but that needed to come out and that made a whole lot of sense and really applied to you. The other thing is, when you're leading a meeting, you develop a sense of responsibility to the people who are in front of you, responding to your leadership.

Listening to Frank talk, I found my commitment to showing up for our guys. My continuing to live right was for them as well, because if I was talking to them about recovery and I relapsed, that could be harmful to them. They could say to themselves, "Man, look at this guy. He seemed to be doing so well. He was talking all that good stuff about recovery, but he still couldn't stay clean. If he can't, what makes me think I can?" That reminded me that maybe everybody else in the world might say that I'm no good because I flunked out of law school, but I knew one thing: there were some recovering addicts who still saw value in me. I still had something to offer, if to nobody else then to the people who were coming through our recovery house trying to stay clean. They were going to see me take a huge hit but keep on ticking. They were going to see me maintain my sobriety through this episode.

# TWELVE

# WOULDN'T IT BE GREAT IF I MADE DEAN'S LIST?

HAD A WEEK LEFT Of my vacation on Saint Croix when I found out I had received a failing grade in Criminal Law. I kept saying to myself, *I'm going to block this out of my mind. I'm going to do all I can to enjoy the last week I have here on this island. When I go home, I'll resolve this. Something has got to be wrong. Maybe that grade really was a mistake. . . .*

I tried my best to enjoy myself, but always in the back of my mind was, *I have some business I have to take care of when I get back to Miami.*

When I finally returned to school, I went straight to see the professor who had given me the F. I remember sitting down in his office. He told me that my answers weren't wrong; they just weren't in the format that he wanted them in.

I was stunned when I heard that. "What does that even mean?" I asked him. "What was the right format?"

It turned out that different professors had different styles of writing they favored. One of the major formats for legal argument is called IRAC: issue, reasoning, analysis, and conclusion. That was the style he favored. The style I wrote in was not the style he liked.

When I was honored at the law school five years after graduating, that same professor approached me and apologized. He said he was wrong. At that moment, though, I was in total disbelief. If I got the right answers, at least give me a C or a D. But to give me an F? F means you didn't try. To give me an F, I thought, was totally unfair. But what could I say?

————————

WHEN I CHOSE A LAW SCHOOL, ONE OF THE REASONS I'D PICKED FLORIDA INTERNATIONAL University was its location in Miami. I thought, *Wouldn't it be poetic for me to graduate law school in the same city where I was at my lowest, where I was contemplating suicide, where I was a homeless crack addict?*

The other reason I picked FIU College of Law was because it was a fairly new school. I truly believed I could be a catalyst in shaping a type of law school that would be a little bit different. My first year, I ran for office and was elected as the 1L (first-year) law student representative. I used my position to try to convince as many of my peers at law school how important community service is. Giving back is even more important when you're a lawyer. We are the last line of defense for the human race. When you can't resolve an issue with somebody, you bring in a lawyer. When you're harmed, you seek out a lawyer. When you're accused of a crime and imprisoned, you ask for a lawyer. When you're looking for compensation for something you feel you earned, you go to a lawyer. A lawyer is that defender of the people, the guardian of civility in our society. With a role that important, I felt there should be an element of community service that's attached to it. When you're defending the people, you really have to understand the people. You've got to really be a part of the community. You have to consider yourself a servant.

We have to treat everybody with dignity and respect. I remember one of the things that I did was for Valentine's Day, when I went around and collected money from as many of my classmates as I could. I bought roses and chocolates for all the female custodians at the law school. I even gave some chocolates to the male custodians. I was the type of person who felt they deserved just as much respect as the dean of the law school would get. It was very important to me that they knew that they were not invisible and to encourage my classmates to remember that these folks clean up after us. They keep our school looking clean, and every now and then we should thank them.

I always made it a point to speak to the custodial staff and to ask how they were doing, to let them know they were no different from me, because at the end of the day, guess what? I had been in a worse position than they were just a few years before. I'm definitely not one to look down on anyone. Those relationships came back to me after I returned from Saint Croix. Even the janitors knew what happened to me, and they were so supportive. They asked me if there was anything they could do on my behalf, anyone they could speak to.

That really touched me, and they were not alone. There were so many people who offered to write me a letter of support. Some of my classmates and professors wrote about how prepared I was for class. That was something I had committed to in undergrad and continued all the way through law school. Have you ever seen the shows where they're depicting law school, and the professor is engaged in the Socratic method? Where he or she calls on somebody and that person is not prepared, and the professor eats them alive? Visions of that haunted me, and one thing my professors would tell you is that I never entered into a classroom without being prepared. If I walk in there, I'm going to be ready to handle the questions.

So a lot of people were shocked and confused that I had been dismissed, because they knew I was always prepared. I was an intelligent guy who helped others with their studies. So how, they wondered, could I have failed? How could I be dismissed? And they wondered if there was anything they could do to get me back in.

I went to the assistant dean of the law school to find out if I had an opportunity to appeal the dismissal or somehow ask for a reconsideration. There was, but it was a long shot. The person in charge of my hearing was actually my Contracts professor from my first semester, so we knew each other. Before the proceedings started, he came out to tell me what to expect. He finished his description of the procedures by telling me that it was harder for someone to get reinstated in law school than for a camel to pass through the eye of a needle. That hit me in a way I will never forget.

Here I was in law school, and the first person I was advocating for was me. In a sense, I had been preparing for this since my first days of undergrad. Then I was fully expecting someone to come tap me on the shoulder and say, "You don't belong here. You're an addict. You're homeless. You have a criminal record." In my head, I was always pleading my case and saying, "Look at the good work I've done. Look at the A's I've gotten. Make an exception for me." I never had to argue that in undergrad, but now I had to speak forcefully, yet humbly, on my own behalf.

I went into the hearing room and pled my case. As it turns out, I wasn't alone. A number of my professors had vouched that I was never unprepared for class. They knew, based on my class participation and level of understanding, that I grasped the legal theories and concepts we were discussing. A few days later, the school informed me they were going to reinstate me on a conditional basis. I wrote letters to everyone on that committee, thanking them for reinstating me and promising to do my best. At the end of each note, I said, "Wouldn't it be fitting that I would go from academic probation to making the Dean's List?" One of the professors with a reputation in the school as being a really tough, no-nonsense educator wrote back and said, "Just get it done." He meant, "Listen, thank you's are all good and fine, but at the end of the day, you need to graduate law school."

Besides being put on academic probation, there were a couple of other stipulations to my return to law school. One was that I undertake some special testing. These tests revealed that I had a high IQ, but that I had a learning disability. In classes where the final exam was multiple choice or fill in the blank, I'd do well. In classes where the exam was a series of written essays, I would struggle. Basically, it was hard for me to take what was in my head and write it down on paper.

That was very revealing. I wondered how I had been able to do so well in my undergraduate studies. It was explained to me that because of my intellectual gifts I had been able to power through them. But law school is so intense, it exposes any flaw that you have. I had gone through life with a learning disability and I didn't even know it. When they were able to give me special accommodations, such as an extra hour on a timed written exam, my test scores rose dramatically. It was like new life was breathed into me. Law school can never be characterized as a cakewalk, but my appreciation for being there kept a smile permanently spread across my face. It was a great honor and privilege to be there, knowing all of the odds that were against me.

I doubled down on my commitment to do my best. I worked even harder on being prepared for class discussion. Most of these discussions are held in the Socratic method, which means you have to do a ton of reading in casebooks for every subject. You not only have to read them, but you have to take notes on the key points so that when you go into class you'll be able to defend one side or the other; you'll be able to actually engage in discussion about legal principles or theories or tactics. If you're talking about anticipatory breach of contract that day, for example, the professor might ask you regarding a case that deals with that: "Well, what did the court say? Why did the court rule that way? Could the court have ruled differently? Why?"

Ever since undergrad, I had believed that whenever I was assigned any work, I started on it right then and there. Now I took that to another level. I was not only prepared; I was ahead of schedule. I knew what pages I had to read to be prepared to discuss them in each class that I had. What I did now was make sure that I had read and briefed— that's what the process of taking notes about the cases is called—the cases all the way up to about two weeks ahead of time. That way, when I had spare time, I could go over my notes one more time before class.

It allowed everything to sink in on another level. At the end of my first semester in my second year, I knocked my exams out of the park. One of the classes I took was the Contracts class I had gotten a C in previously. Because of the stipulations of my probation, I had to take that class again and this time I got an A. Everywhere, those As and Bs started coming in. I never got anything lower than a B again.

AS THE YEARS WENT ON, I GOT MORE FLEXIBILITY IN THE TYPE OF CLASSES I COULD TAKE in law school. There were clinics designed to assist people who could not afford attorneys who had certain specialties, and I was able to take one of those.

One of the classes that I remember vividly from the end of my time at law school was Trial Advocacy, which taught people how to prepare for and conduct a trial. We were given a fictitious case. Some of us were the defense, representing a person charged with a crime; some of us played the role of the state, prosecuting the accused. They gave us the facts and some evidence. We had to take that material and, without making anything up, figure out how we were going to either prosecute this person or defend them. I was assigned to be the defense attorney for a lady who was accused of killing her married lover. Throughout the semester, I put my case together. We were taught how to give an opening and closing statement, when and where to object, what the legal reasoning was behind certain objections. These were things I'd seen on *Perry Mason* all those years before, but now it was becoming real life for me.

The final exam was to conduct the actual trial in a courtroom. We were to be graded on how well we examined the witnesses, either by helping our own witnesses to express themselves in beneficial ways or by cross-examining the witnesses of the opposition. Of special importance was whether we could give a closing argument without reading from notes. We would be in front of a real judge, with a jury made up of other assistant state attorneys or assistant state defenders. That room would be full of people who do this for a living, which added to the pressure we all felt. My pressure was particularly enhanced by the fact that our final exam was going to be at the Miami-Dade County Courthouse, where I had spent some time in my past life.

The day of the final exam was a Saturday. In the morning, we headed to the courthouse. They assigned us a courtroom randomly, from thirty to forty possible courtrooms. Everything was going as planned until we got to the point of the trial where both sides rest their case. Then the (pretend) state went first with its closing argument.

The state stands in front of the jury, talking to them. What typically happens is, because each side has these big poster boards where they lay out their case, the rest of us would move over and sit next to the jury box, to see what the state is showing the jury in case we need to object to something. Sometimes you might object even when you know you may not win, but the objection might be impactful or strategic.

I moved over there and sat down, although I wasn't planning on objecting to anything. I was just trying to rehearse my own closing statement to myself. I didn't want to get points knocked off by going up there with a piece of paper in my hand. I happened to look up and noticed that on the opposite side of the courtroom, behind where I was previously sitting as the defense attorney, there was a picture hanging on the wall. When I looked at the picture more closely, I saw it was a picture of this judge named Manny Crespo, who had passed away. This courtroom, which used to be his, was now dedicated to him. It was at that moment that I felt like the roof caved in on me.

What I realized at that moment was that I was actually in the same courtroom where, in 2001, I had stood before that very judge. They used to call him Let-'Em-Go-Crespo, because he was known to be lenient. Well, he wasn't that day. I remember his exact words: "The people of Dade County have spoken. As a result, I remand you to the custody of the Florida Department of Corrections for 15 years." When he said that, my knees buckled. What flashed through my mind was, *My life is over. Desmond is done. I'm going to spend the rest of my life in prison.* It was only fifteen years, but that is an eternity to a man in his prime.

Now there I was, sitting as a law student in the same courtroom where I had been sentenced to fifteen years. My mind went totally blank, until the voice of the judge pierced through: "Defense, are you ready?"

What do I say? *Judge, right now, I'm having a moment. I don't know anything.* Everything had disappeared. The only thing that came out of my mouth was, "Yes, Your Honor." I had to walk in front of the jury with these thoughts still in my head. I couldn't remember my closing argument. I was stuck.

I stood in front of the jury and I looked at each and every one of them, one by one, stalling while I tried to remember the beginning of my argument. The only thing that came back to me was that I was going to show them the palm of my hand and say, "If I were to ask you what you were looking at, chances are you would say that you were looking at my hand." And after I said that, I was going to twist my hand back and forth and show them both the back of my hand and the palm of my hand, and say, "But that would not be entirely accurate. Just like this story, the hand has two sides. Just like this case, there's two sides to the story."

After I put my palm out, it all came flooding back to me. I went into the zone. I banged out a killer closing statement. It was a drop-the-mic moment. After the end of the trial, I went over to my professor and told him what happened. He said, "My gosh, Desmond, why didn't you say something? We could have made a different arrangement." I said, "No, it's good. It's all good."

I left the courtroom and got in my car. I called Sheena and started crying. I was crying remembering being in that courtroom and thinking that my life was over almost exactly fifteen years ago. Now, here I was, as a law student, in the very same courtroom, arguing a case the same year I would have been scheduled to be released if I had served the entire fifteen-year sentence

Of all the courtrooms in that building, of all the places to sit in that courtroom, that this was how things unfolded amazed me to the core. If that was not God showing me that there is some purpose for me, I don't know what would be. I don't know what other explanation you could offer. I took that as a sign that I was heading in the right direction, to keep doing the things I was doing, to keep feeling the things I was feeling. It was one enormous confirmation.

When I had graduated from college, I remembered pausing for a moment before walking across the stage to get my diploma. I stood there because I wanted to give my mother in heaven a chance to bask in that. My mom's belief in education was a driving, if belated, motivation for me to finish school. When she died, I wasn't all the way right. I was a drug addict. I felt like I didn't make her proud the way I had planned to when I was a little kid. I had missed that opportunity before, so I had to take advantage of it now.

When I graduated from law school, I paused on stage in a similar fashion. But this time, it was not just for my mom. This time it was for every person who's ever had a felony conviction. For every person who's ever been addicted to drugs or alcohol. For every person who's ever been homeless. For every person who's ever been told they won't amount to anything. I walked across the stage for all of those folks, and I wanted the audience to see it. There were parents in the audience who had sons and daughters who were incarcerated or had disappeared into the wilds of addiction. I wanted to show the world that in spite of the mistakes we may have made, in spite of the situations that seem hopeless, there is hope. There is an opportunity to accomplish great things. I had made the Dean's List in my final year after all. And now I was going into the world with my doctor of jurisprudence degree.

# THIRTEEN

# THE GREATEST INDICATOR
# OF CITIZENSHIP

THE MOCK TRIAL at the end of law school connected to me and my experiences, and it helped create in me a resolve that I was going to need. When all the experts and all the consultants said that restoring the rights of felons in Florida was impossible, that experience in the courtroom played a role in my having the type of faith that believes it doesn't matter what people say. A judge says to me you're going to be incarcerated for fifteen years—I believed it myself at the time, but God didn't. There was something bigger at play here. I was walking in my purpose. Others might not see it, because it was a personal mission. My whole family might not understand it. But there was a burden that I alone, and no one else, had to carry and real hope that I could clearly see and believe in.

DURING THE NEXT SIX YEARS, THE FLORIDA RIGHTS RESTORATION COALITION GOT HELP from so many sources that it was humbling. The PICO (People Improving Communities Through Organizing) National Network and their Florida branch, Live Free (Lifelines to Healing), the ACLU, the Advancement Project, the Florida Justice League, the Brennan Center for Justice, the NAACP, the Sentencing Project, the League of Women Voters, DEMOS—every one of these organizations contributed some thinking to what a ballot initiative to re-enfranchise returning citizens could look like.

All I knew before receiving input from these groups was that I was directly impacted by disenfranchisement, that felon disenfranchisement was not good for our state, and that we needed to do something to change the policies maintaining it. I had the content for making the case for re-enfranchisement, but I was sorely lacking in the mechanisms for how to get it done. A constitutional amendment on a statewide ballot would not stand a chance without substantive input from anyone who had something of value to add. Whether someone contributed funds for research, access to a phone bank, help with canvassing, or just a thought-provoking conversation, it was all welcome to me.

I guess one of my contributions was to be humble enough to let it all in. But how could I not be? For much of that time, while I was in school, in addition to managing the three-quarter-way house, I was working as a short-order cook. I didn't know what these other folks knew. Come to think of it, my hospitality experience is a good example of not only my own arc but also of movement building.

Before I was first released from the drug treatment program, I got help retrieving documents like my birth certificate and my Social Security card. You need that identification to get a job, even though there are so many places, too many places, that turn away from hiring returning citizens. According to those employers, there is only one right answer to the question, "Have you ever been convicted of a felony?" You need someone to take a chance on you, which is what a chef at the Hyatt in downtown Miami did.

I applied for a job to be a cook there. I was not a cook. I remember the chef said, "You can cook, huh?" I said, "Yes." He took me in the kitchen, and he put a pan on the stove and said, "Make me some over easy." I tried to do it. I messed the egg up. He gave me four more chances. At that time, he could tell that no, I was not a cook. But there was something about me that he was attracted to.

He said, "You know what? I'm going to give you a chance. I'm going to hire you, but I'm going to train you." He would make me stand in the kitchen in slow periods, and I would have to put a piece of bread in the frying pan and I would have to flip the bread without the bread leaving the frying pan. The bread had to maintain contact with the surface of the frying pan. He kept having me do that.

Once I mastered that, my confidence level started to grow, and I was able to get a job at Denny's as a short-order cook. Denny's may not impress you, but that place is hard work. You have to have it together, and you have to keep it together. Denny's has a fast pace; you had to learn how to be orderly in the kitchen and how to clean as you go. Not doing these things contributes to the kitchen being backed up and you being lost in the weeds. I became a really good cook working there, but when I look at the beginning, I didn't know what I was doing. I was like those penguins in the movie *Madagascar* who were building the plane as they flew it.

It was the same thing with running the ballot initiative. I'd never done anything like this, or even close to this, in my life, but I knew I could figure it out, especially with the kind of help I was getting.

IN 2012, OUR FRRC CONVENING WAS HELD IN ORLANDO. IT WAS THERE THAT I FIRST CAME into contact with People Improving Communities through Organizing (PICO). They were very interested in the restoration of civil rights because some of their leaders in the Orlando area were directly impacted. They had done a listening session with their folks, and they kept hearing about felon disenfranchisement. They were thoroughly impressed with the convening, and that led to me being able to leave Denny's to work for PICO. PICO was the largest organizer of faith-based institutions in the country, whether Christian or Jewish or Islamic or other denominations. I was brought on in Florida to help organize churches, and from that experience I developed a deep bank of connections that would later greatly assist with the ballot initiative.

My work with PICO helped in other ways too. The PICO National Network was running a campaign at the time called Let My People Vote. The phrase "Let my people vote" was actually first used by Pastor Kenneth Glasgow, a formerly incarcerated person and an advocate for criminal justice and voting reform. He labored for years to enfranchise returning citizens throughout the Southern states. PICO's project was specifically designed to get more churches engaged in the voting process, by getting their congregations registered to vote and encouraging them to actively go and vote at the polls. They were using in their flyers and banners an image of a man whose hands were bound by a flag with that wording, "Let My People Vote." That combination of image and text really struck me, and the thought that the phrase originated from a fellow returning citizen and advocate was fitting.

I decided I was going to use that image on the pledge cards that FRRC was designing. The idea behind the pledge cards was to get returning citizens to get five to ten family members and friends to pledge to vote on their behalf. The cards read "I pledge my support to ____," and then the person filled in the name of the returning citizen who couldn't vote, along with the person's name, telephone number, and address. The returning citizen would collect those cards and send them back to me, and we would start building a database of people who were pledging to vote on behalf of their loved ones. I was able to get the pledge cards printed and was soon passing them out as I traveled the state, meeting with returning citizens and anyone who would stop long enough to listen to my pitch.

I also had assistance in printing and distributing these pledge cards from my sister-in-law, Salandra Benton, the state convener for the Florida Coalition on Black Civic Participation. This speaks to something I have seen time and again in my activist life: women are more likely to be engaged than men. This is just my personal observation, but it seems that whatever meeting I might be attending, the majority of the people there were women. Throughout my process most of the folks that were with me, especially when no one else believed that what I was doing was going to go anywhere, were women. Women have really stepped up in a major way in my eyes.

There was no more special example of this than my mother-in-law. As I mentioned earlier, I met Ms. Jackson, or, as everyone affectionately calls her, "Big Ma," months before I met my wife, Sheena. She happened to attend a breakout session where I spoke about felon disenfranchisement. This was not a hot topic at the time, so I was given the last speaking slot of the session. By the time I had my chance to speak, most of attendees had already left the room. Big Ma was one of the few people who remained to listen, and when I was done, she patiently waited as other people lined up to speak with me to share their stories or ask additional questions. By the time we got a chance to speak, I had run out of my makeshift business cards, and she had to write my contact information on a piece of paper.

Among Big Ma's many roles to come was to prepare large mailing envelopes for any packets of blank petitions (once we had graduated from pledge cards) that had to be mailed out to a volunteer, or signed petitions that needed to be mailed to a Supervisor of Elections' office. But her primary role, and the one she loved the best, was sorting out the signed petitions and grouping them by county. She would have large folding tables throughout her living room with mounds of petitions on each one. The living room became her command center, where she could comfortably sort out petitions while watching her Lifetime shows. Big Ma was so committed to her role that when the campaign got to the stage where we had to quickly collect a million petitions and finally had funding to hire staff, it was extremely hard to get her to accept the fact that our now established operations had to take over handling the petitions. She did not go quietly.

Just as there was a time when I was educated and buoyed by so many organizations, there came a time when the running of the campaign seemed to be more of a family operation than anything. When it became apparent that funding was not going to come, the support of organizations waned, and I was left to fend for myself; my wife, five kids, and my mother-in-law were pressed into filling the void left by organizations. It was not too difficult for people from these other organizations to walk away from the campaign when they already had the right to vote, or when they or a loved one was not feeling the weight of collateral consequences because of a felony conviction, but I couldn't just walk away. While everyone could just go back to what they were doing before and still be able to vote the next day, I had nothing to lose by sticking with it, but I had everything to gain. So I stayed, and I sacrificed.

Freshly married, I remember being in the living room with my wife, at times upset and overwhelmed. People ask Sheena now, "How did you guys make it?" And she says, "Well, we just couldn't give up at the same time."

The days I was having a bad day, thinking, *Why am I doing this?*, she would remind me, "Baby, God called you to do this." And then there would be days when she would ask, "Desmond, why are you doing this, with no money and no support?" And I would have to answer, "Honey, I've been called to this, and it's about more than just me."

Sheena says, in the language of our faith, that God had to strip me all the way down, to make sure we knew that no one did this but God. God gave me the strength and ability and endurance to push his campaign along.

AS WE STARTED TO MAKE SOME HEADWAY WITH THE PLEDGE CARDS, THE QUESTION became, What are we asking these supporters to vote for? They are pledging their support, but we don't have any legislation up. There is no focus to our initiative. Politicians are certainly not addressing issues that directly impact returning citizens. Felon re-enfranchisement was a huge topic to be covered with one particular vote. We needed some specificity.

I started to get glimmers of this when I was traveling the state. Almost every community I visited faced the same challenges, exemplified best perhaps by the Parramore community of Orlando. Residents there have suffered tremendously from institutionalized racism. Unemployment there was at nearly 25 percent (and this was long before COVID-19), and median household income hovered just below the poverty line. I got to meet some of the neighborhood's leaders and realize the gravity of their situation. At the same time, so many of them couldn't vote to change any policies that might be affecting their economic well-being. There were even pastors there who couldn't vote.

I remember reading and hearing stories about how, during the civil rights era, when it was time to vote, parents would dress up the family in their finest clothes to go to the polling location. Voting was a festive occasion, and civic participation was a part of many discussions held at the dinner table. But like the saying goes, "If you cut off the head of a snake, the rest of the body will die," so when fathers, mothers, and preachers are stripped of the right to vote, it killed those conversations at the dinner table and at community gatherings, and the enthusiasm to participate in democracy on a larger scale died right along with it. That was an inspiration for FRRC, to land on the best way to begin the process of the re-enfranchisement of all rights for returning citizens. We would start with the right to vote.

All rights are important to returning citizens: to be able to surpass occupational license restrictions or housing restrictions or education restrictions; to serve on a jury; to run for office; and to own a firearm. All of these make up an individual's civil rights. But when I looked at all of those rights, the one that stuck out more than any other was the right to vote. I had learned over the course of the years since returning from prison that nothing speaks more to citizenship than being able to have your voice heard. If we were limited to just dealing with one issue at a time, that seemed like the single most important civil right. Nothing restores dignity more effectively than the right to vote, which in turn can lead to all kinds of other positive momentum for an individual.

Once we decided on the heart of our ballot initiative, we were able to undertake another round of polling with the assistance of the Brennan Center. We were still reeling a little bit from the polls in the previous decade that showed an overwhelming number of voters against the restoration of returning citizens' rights. Now we wanted to dig a little deeper and figure out why. What's going on in the minds of voters?

We did focus groups throughout the state of Florida: one in the Orlando area, two in the Jacksonville area, and two in the Miami area. Each group was made up of a different set of demographics. We found out a few things of distinct interest. The first was that people were strongly opposed to restoring voting rights to people who were convicted of crimes like murder, child molestation, and rape. The second thing we found out was that people were more inclined to be supportive of the restoration of voting rights when someone had completed all portions of their sentence, not just when they were released from prison. Folks wanted to make sure that those who were on probation or parole had completed their sentence before having their voting rights restored.

I was fortunate enough to attend four out of the five focus groups, and one of the things I felt strongly was that people there did believe in redemption. They did believe in restoration as a matter of moral principle. How that happened just had to be crafted the right way. So we took the findings from the focus groups and went back to the drawing board. We carved out those convicted of homicide, sexual crimes, or crimes against children, and we introduced the stipulation that a returning citizen must have completed all of their post-release obligations. When we did that, the support for restoration skyrocketed. I had heard that no one was going to support a ballot initiative unless you could show polls that were at least 60 percent in favor of it, which was the threshold needed for such an effort to pass. The reasoning went that there are things that will happen that make your numbers go down, and all of your work can help them rise again, but your initial number has to be there. Well, our initial number was 77 percent in support of our initiative.

When we got that number back, my heart just jumped. I didn't want to get too excited too fast, but I couldn't help it. I just felt like, *Oh my God, we have a pathway*. I maintained my composure, but I couldn't believe what I was seeing. I knew this would excite folks working for our cause and provide an infusion of optimism. With this research backing us up, funders were going to turn out. There might be periods of doubt ahead for others, but there were not going to be any more dark days for me, because deep down inside I already knew what the research eventually told us: most people care about, and believe in, forgiveness and giving people second chances.

# FOURTEEN

# NO MAN IS AN ISLAND

W**HILE THERE WERE** plenty of times I felt alone in my journey, the reality is that there was no way Amendment 4 would have been
successful if it were not for the countless volunteers who poured their
hearts into the campaign—even before it officially became a campaign. There were literally hundreds of people from Pensacola to Key
West and all points in between who, in spite of the odds being against
us, continued to support me and the effort. It would be impossible for
me to remember all of the names. It would take another book just to
talk about the ones I do remember, but I have tried to mention here
the major forces of support. In that context, I have to mention Pastor
McBride of the Live Free Campaign as the first person who invested
in me and the one who invested in me the most.

Not too long after I started working for PICO, I met Michael Mc-
Bride. He was a pastor and the director of a campaign called Live
Free, which at the time was called Lifelines to Healing. Whenever I
introduced myself as president of the Florida Rights Restoration Coalition, people naturally thought that I was employed. They thought
I was getting a paycheck when I wasn't. I was surviving off of my
student loans for college and then for law school.

When Pastor McBride heard I was working for PICO, he said,
"Wait a minute, I didn't even know you were looking for a job. I want
you with Live Free."

I said, "I want to rock with anybody who wants to rock with me."

Pastor McBride's reputation preceded him. He was a powerful man who was part of a powerful organization; if you had them behind you, you definitely had a leg up. At the same time, he had style. My first glimpse of him revealed that: a man of the cloth who wore a suit, yet he paired that with white Air Force 1 tennis shoes à la Reverend Run from Run DMC. He was able to connect with a wide range of age groups while articulating the issues that were really important. Every moment that I spent with him, I became even more inspired. He did his work as a young African American clergy member with such passion. You could easily sense there was a deep commitment to really improving the lives of Black and Brown people, and he had a spirit that made it pleasant to be around him.

What I didn't know was that he had already heard about me from someone in his organization. They asked me to come in and share my story while they took some photographs. I didn't realize that my outlook would have an impact on the policymakers who were higher up. He was impressed with how I carried myself and wanted to know more about me.

I was able to share with him my dreams about the work I wanted to do in Florida around returning-citizen disenfranchisement. He affirmed his belief in where I was trying to go and wanted to take the necessary steps to support that work. He created a space for me to be able to do my FRRC work while also working for him as the state director for the Live Free Campaign in Florida. I'm eternally grateful to him for that. That space allowed me to focus attention on taking the next strategic steps that previously had just been rolling around in my head.

I told him, "Listen, I'm going to do all that I can, so whoever may have doubted your decision to bring me on is going to know that you made the right choice, that you have vision. I'm going to make you look as smart as I possibly can."

The work of Live Free dealt with gun violence, reducing mass incarceration, and other issues that have directly impacted African American communities. Even though I was focused on rights restoration, I couldn't escape the reality of the way everything worked together. I got to see firsthand the connection between gun violence and felon disenfranchisement.

Say that a guy gets out of prison. Originally, he was arrested for selling drugs; he goes to prison, he gets out of prison. Once he gets out of prison, he can't get a good job, can't get an education, can't live where he wants to live; he's ostracized by his own community. What is he going to do? He's going to go back to selling drugs. If he's selling drugs, eventually, at some point he is going to get a gun to protect himself against people who are either trying to rob him or from rival dope sellers. And now the thing about this guy is, he's not ex-military. He doesn't have any formal gun training, but at some point he's going to end up using that gun. He's going to shoot and, because he doesn't know how to shoot straight, everybody's going to get hit but the person who he was really shooting at, and you have innocent people dying. He's causing trauma to so many other people, and we can trace that all back to the fact that when he was released from prison, he didn't want to go back to being a drug dealer. He wanted to live a decent life, but because all of these avenues were cut off, he was forced back into this environment. This is the life that he was forced to live.

Live Free provided that connection to the point where I often didn't feel like I was working on two separate issues. They both have a direct connection to the community, and I could work on them simultaneously. Even though I was focused on the restoration of rights, because gun violence surrounded me, there was a part of me that had to fight for the bigger picture. There were people dying every day. Every day I would go through my social media feed or wake up to hear a story on the news about somebody who was killed. A lot of times it was young Black or Brown men who were victims of a drive-by shooting here.

There were so many times when I was driving throughout the state of Florida, from one city to the next, that I would hear something on the news: A shooting in Miami. A shooting in Orlando. And I would just start crying. I used to cry a lot when I traveled. There's just so much time to think. Every time I was hit with a new account of something bad that was happening to African Americans, I thought, *Wow, I don't know of any race of people in the United States that have to deal with getting gunned down, or getting into altercations with police that don't end well, or getting arrested and convicted and getting disenfranchised on a daily basis. All of the things that are happening to Black folks in this country, aren't happening with nearly the same prevalence to other races. If this were to happen to a race of people in another country, we would be accusing that country of genocide.*

The most frustrating part about it was that people would react with grief and anger—there might even be a rally about it—but then it always went back to business as usual. Another young Black man was shot down in the street? Wow, that's bad. But it would never quite capture the interest and commitment of policymakers to stop the violence.

As part of my work with Live Free, I was able to travel to Ohio to meet Michelle Alexander, who had written *The New Jim Crow: Mass Incarceration in the Age of Colorblindness.* I was so excited to get to meet her and have my picture taken with her because reading her book was like reading about my life. It was full of people who had been locked behind bars and then denied the very rights we thought we had won back in the 1960s. We know that there's over-policing in African American communities. We know that African Americans are disproportionately arrested because of that over-policing and disproportionately convicted. So then you have a greater percentage of the African American community losing their civil rights as compared to a similarly situated white community. Before the emergence of Black Lives Matter, before the murders of Trayvon Martin, Mike Brown, and Sandra Bland, race relations in this country had never been adequately addressed. Implicit racial bias and explicit racial tensions have always been there, even as they were covered over or conveniently overlooked by other distractions or our unwillingness as a country to address it. When Barack Obama was first elected president, we expected that to be a moment when race relations made a turn for the better. Some folks say racism died the night President Obama delivered his "Yes, We Can" acceptance speech onstage in Chicago. But there was no appreciable turn for the better. Racism did not die, and movements like Black Lives Matter dragged this ugly truth to the surface for the world to see.

Some days I felt like I could work on both issues at the same time, and other days I was torn. Looking at the activists who have tried to beat the drum about the issues impacting African Americans just like me, there was a strong compulsion to want to dive into that. But I knew that to do it right I would have to give it 100 percent of my attention. That would naturally take away from the work I was doing with felon disenfranchisement, which was the real work I was called to do. It hurt, because my people were hurting. No campaign exists in the abstract. There are always the stresses of everything else that's happening in our community or our country, every single day. Nonetheless, I felt like all of the signs kept calling me back to felon disenfranchisement, reminding me not to let go of my particular role to play in the grander vision.

Live Free gave me opportunities to go all around the country to see the type of work that they were doing to end gun violence. Before, my experience had always been in the state of Florida, where I never passed up an opportunity to talk to returning citizens and hear their personal stories. Now I was able to see all kinds of different programs from coast to coast, and that exposure helped me mature. I met returning citizens who were doing amazing work in their respective states, fighting for the rights and dignity of people with felony convictions, particularly people who had been incarcerated. To this day, I look at many of these people as mentors. They are the ones I bounce ideas off of, or from whom I take direction, using the programs and initiatives they've implemented within their state or organization to build the FRRC of today.

In retrospect, Live Free played a significant role in developing the DNA of the Florida Rights Restoration Coalition. My time with both Live Free and PICO helped give me a better sense of what we could do with FRRC. We were in the middle of direct actions, marches, and protests, as well as election work and public education work. When I was in Miami, my advocacy was in the form of going to board meetings, giving input into policy discussions, holding homeless memorials, things of that nature. I didn't understand the power dynamics, I didn't understand about issue cutting, and I didn't understand about how to leverage money and people. I learned all of that working with Live Free and PICO.

It all came down to the fact that people have the power to come together and convince elected officials to do the things we need them to do. Being an elected official means being a public servant; they serve their constituents, the voters. What successful business do you know where the boss has to beg an employee to do something and when the employee doesn't do it, they still get a promotion or even a raise? What hampers basic organizing practices today is the fact that we have turned public servants into demigods, and their constituents are walking around as if they're servants. You have a group of individuals who voted to elect a certain person into office, but when they need to speak to that person, they get the runaround. They rarely get to see that person in their office. If they do get an appointment, nine times out of ten, it turns out they are speaking with the pol's chief of staff or a low-level aide and not the elected official. But you can guarantee that if that elected official's biggest donor were to say he wanted to speak to him or her, that elected official would probably even go to that donor.

At the end of the day, that one donor should not trump the thousands of constituents who also voted for this person. A lot of folks accept this as commonplace, but that was not the original intention when this country was formed, and it's not a conducive mindset to have when you're organizing. That realization allowed me to be comfortable with saying that there's no way we were going to ask, or even allow, an elected official to endorse our campaign. If you're the boss, you need to act like the boss. With our cause, that's the mindset we had. We acted like we were the boss. We didn't rely on a politician for anything. We were going to show what people power truly looks like.

A great example of that was the work that Mila Al-Ayoubi and I did together. As a result of the positive polling on felon disenfranchisement, Pastor McBride was able to convince PICO to allow Mila, who eventually became our program administrator, to work with me. Remember in law school when it was discovered I had a learning disability? That learning disability basically indicated that while I had a high IQ, I had trouble taking things that were in my head and actually putting them on paper. Mila's job was basically to take the vision that I had about the ballot initiative and operationalize it.

Mila was a driving force behind a 2012 campaign to defeat a constitutional amendment that was on the ballot around taxes. She put together and executed the plan to defeat what was called Amendment

3 in that election year. She was hard-core, and I knew if we were going to succeed we would need someone who knew what they were doing and was no nonsense.

We didn't have a fundraising plan at the time. Mila put together our first real proposal and began shopping it around. We were constantly tweaking it, going back and forth, going through scenarios. Many times we were up late at night on the phone fussing with each other; we'd call it quits, and the next day, we were right back to trying to move this thing forward.

We got advice to go to the Ballot Initiative Strategy Center conference. That's sort of the clearinghouse of ballot initiatives, where you can connect with people and find out all of the current best practices. We weren't part of the in-crowd there, however. When you talk about these campaigns, you see the same people running them year after year. Even if they have a history of losing, it's still the same leaders. These leaders would bring on consultants who they have relationships with, so you find the same consultants on every campaign as well. It was like a social club that didn't allow other people in.

Well, I didn't want our campaign to be the same old regular campaign. I didn't think our campaign was regular. In order for us to get money to further our work, however, funders were insistent that we hire a seasoned person to put together a campaign plan for us. We eventually agreed and hired a professional campaign person. But what was the final product from that campaign person who we paid a lot of money? The exact same plan that Mila had already written. Mila and I had a different way of doing things, one that people resisted because they were so used to doing things a certain way. We broke that mold. And over time, we got the funders to accept us and to acknowledge that the work we were doing was quality work.

THIS WAS AROUND THE TIME THAT OUR PREVIOUS PARTNERS STARTED COMING BACK TO FRRC. One of the things these organizations had taught me was that people need validators, and I had to be strategic about providing motivation for them to get excited again about our mission. Needing third-party validation is either human nature or a necessary evil; I'm not sure which. You might have the greatest idea in the world, but sometimes the folks you are trying to convince to support that idea need to know that somebody else supports it. They could think it's a great idea, too, but they are going to ask, "Well, what about (this other organization)? How do they feel about it?"

One of the first validators that I pursued was the Alliance for Safety and Justice, because they had just won a ballot initiative, Proposition 47, in California, which reclassified certain low-level felonies into misdemeanors. I thought if I could get somebody with that kind of credibility, someone who had been to the mountaintop, as it were, to say that our ballot initiative had potential, that would draw others in. The alliance was very interested. They came on board immediately, which felt like we had just taken a giant step forward.

Prop 47 was an amazing ballot initiative that impacted people's lives, but it was confined within the borders of one state. When you looked at our ballot initiative, I would tell people, its impact would transcend the borders of Florida, because Florida has always played a key role in the outcome of national elections. To be able to re-enfranchise over a million and a half returning citizens and add them to the voting roster would have a significant impact on moving forward.

We now tried to leverage our newfound momentum to pursue funding on a higher level. At the time, I didn't understand the intricate and sometimes delicate interplay between funders and the grassroots. That is something I came to realize during the later stages of the process, when it turned out that canvassing, grassroots campaigning, and word-of-mouth were just as valuable to our efforts as relationships with funders. I quickly learned that, as with a typical ballot initiative, our efforts were going to be very expensive, and fundraising was most definitely going to be a key element of our success.

I didn't have a relationship with any funders. I was relying on others to have those conversations. I was moving forward on faith that those conversations were happening, that people were going to see the potential of the work that we were doing, and that people were going to invest. When the time finally came for me to get on some of these calls, I learned something else quickly . . . and, I suppose we would say, the hard way.

I remember it vividly. We were talking to a potential major funder about putting this amendment on the ballot for 2016, which was still at this time a few years away.

The funder asked, "If Hillary Clinton's people do not want the amendment to be on the ballot in 2016, would you be willing to stop?"

I was still a little rusty on protocol, I guess. I blurted out, "No! Why would we stop because somebody doesn't want it? This is for the people!"

What I didn't know at the time, when I said, "No, that we would not be willing to stop," was that I had signed the death warrant for the ballot initiative in that year, because there were folks in the Hillary Clinton camp who believed that having something like this on the ballot would be hurtful to her campaign for president. We can see in hindsight that the machine built around Hillary stifled anything they viewed as a threat to her candidacy. Our ballot initiative fell into that category, because they calculated that it was an issue that would be decided along partisan lines. They believed that Republicans would be dead set against it, and that would rally turnout of people who would also vote for their candidate for president. That would hurt the Clinton campaign. So when I said that we would not stop, that set in motion a series of conversations that restricted, or actually completely shut off, any funding that was headed our way.

FIFTEEN

# COOKING UP SOME GUMBO

MY EXPERIENCE WITH the Clinton campaign brought home again how racialized this issue was in the minds of many of the uninformed. That meant that anybody who didn't care about African American men or, let's put it a different way, who didn't feel as much commitment toward addressing the explicit or implicit racial biases that African Americans have had to endure in this country, are not likely to be supportive of rights restoration. The statistics didn't support felony disenfranchisement as a purely African American issue, but perception did, and we all know which one of those two is going to prove more important.

THAT RACIALIZATION OF OUR BALLOT INITIATIVE WAS THE NEXT HURDLE WE HAD TO FACE, and it was a large one. In a state like Florida, we would need more than just African Americans to support the issue.

How did it get this way? When people thought about felon disenfranchisement, they thought about crime. They thought about people coming out of prison. If you close your eyes and think of criminal justice, the image that you see is more often than not one of an African American person. For some people, that's because they know about the disproportionate impact that felon disenfranchisement has on the African American community. They know the history of how felon disenfranchisement targeted the newly freed slaves. But for the majority of folks out there, when the image of a felon pops up in their minds, it is an African American man, because that's what society has ingrained in us.

The math, however, doesn't support this conclusion. The statistics fluctuate, but it tends to average that only one in four individuals who commit a felony is African American. What feeds the false narrative that African Americans are the overwhelming number of people who commit felonies it that it is African Americans who are far more likely to be imprisoned for their crime. In that sense, felon re-enfranchisement would very much help repair the fabric of the African American community, with so many Black men and women getting out of jail.

But those aren't the only people who lose their rights—everyone who is convicted of a felony loses their right to vote, to serve on a jury, to own a firearm, and so forth. Public perception of felon disenfranchisement as an African American issue is formed, however, by the fact that 75 percent of people who are convicted of felony offenses in a given year are not sentenced to prison. Most of those offenders are white, with more money, better access to quality legal services, and the benefit of a perception that causes judges and juries alike to overlook troubling aspects of their cases.

How could we separate the painful fact that African Americans are disproportionate represented in the prison population and highlight how felony disenfranchisement actually impacts folks across not only racial demographics but across political demographics as well? It is not a partisan issue. It is not an African American issue. It is an all-American issue.

THE FACT THAT THIS WAS A HUMAN ISSUE, AND DID NOT BELONG PARTICULARLY TO ONE group or another, became the most important consideration for how we shaped our messaging going forward. We learned there was a science to this work and brought in the renowned psychologist Dr. Phyllis Watts. Bringing her into the fold elevated our discussions about how voters think and react. Dr. Watts was able to fairly quickly identify certain elements that could trigger racial anxieties in the psychology of a voter. At the time, it reminded me of a book I read, *Dog Whistle Politics: How Coded Racial Appeals Have Reinvented Racism and*

*Wrecked the Middle Class.* In that text, the author, Ian Haney López, identified multiple examples from our nation's history of politicians making racially based appeals without ever identifying the groups they were demonizing. In those cases, politicians were trying to convince white voters that minorities were their true enemies.

We wanted to avoid using language that would trigger a primal response from voters. Instead, we wanted to use language to educate voters as to all of the positives that felon re-enfranchisement would generate. For example, if you restore civil rights to people, that can stimulate the economy and expand the tax-paying base. It can reduce crime, which not only increases public safety but also translates into savings for the state and the ability to relocate dollars to other areas of need.

A CITIZENS' INITIATIVE TO CHANGE THE STATE CONSTITUTION IS REQUIRED TO DEAL with only one subject at a time. Even if it inadvertently dealt with something else, the initiative stood the chance of being ruled unconstitutional. This is contrary to what the Florida Constitution Revision Commission could do, which was to lump two or even three different issues together into one proposed amendment. Those issues might not be even related to each other; there could be an amendment that deals with the schools, the courts, and the environment all at the same time. A voter might only agree with one of the three issues, but they would have to vote for all three of them in order to get the one they want approved.

As we fine-tuned our single-pointed ballot initiative, we had a lot of considerations to juggle. There was everything we had found in our second set of polling to take into account; we wanted our language to mirror the responses of focus groups that had resulted in such enthusiastic numbers. A cohort of us drafted samples, running them by other organizations as well as attorneys and judges. I saw us getting closer and closer to actually landing on the final wording, where we had dotted all our i's and crossed all our t's—and shredded all those other what-ifs.

One of the challenges of proposing a constitutional amendment is that you only get a certain number of words to put on the ballot.

You could have a longer text that is available to voters in a booklet provided by the Florida Division of Elections. But on the ballot itself, including the title, the description could only be seventy-five words long. You also can't engage in electioneering, meaning you can't tie your initiative to the candidacy of any individual running for local, state, or federal office.

There were some concerns about whether or not we would be in alignment with the single-subject rule. We considered trying to address that by having multiple initiatives. For instance, the Fair Districts Campaign, a measure to limit gerrymandered districts so that politicians are less able to protect their seats by rewarding their allies, had to present two amendments: Amendment 5 and Amendment 6. They both passed in 2010, but if only one had, the other would have been irretrievably weakened. We didn't want to risk dividing people's support that way, and also, two initiatives cost, if not twice the money, at least a lot more than one did.

We decided to just be as simple as possible and focus on restoring the ability to vote. It took us over a year, but eventually we came up with language for the Voting Restoration Amendment in October of 2014 that we felt comfortable with:

> This amendment restores the voting rights of Floridians with felony convictions after they complete all terms of their sentence including parole or probation. The amendment would not apply to those convicted of murder or sexual offenses, who would continue to be permanently barred from voting unless the Governor and Cabinet vote to restore their voting rights on a case by case basis.

We submitted the language to the Florida secretary of state and waited. The process after that would be as follows: If our language was approved, we would then put it on a petition. After we collected a certain number of petitions in a certain number of congressional districts, that would trigger a review by the Florida Supreme Court. That review would analyze the initiative to see if it met all of the legal requirements. If the opinion was favorable, we would be allowed to continue to collect petitions until we had the required number to get it onto the ballot and put it before voters.

So there would be many moments of truth, but this was our first one. The secretary of state came back with an approval. It was game on. On October 31, 2014, I printed the first batch of petitions to be collected. Now we would have to use our hearts and understanding to bring that language to the people.

PART OF THAT MISSION FELL TO ME. I HAVE A LONG HISTORY OF BEING ABLE TO CROSS the barriers erected by race. My earliest memory, in fact, on Saint Croix, was about my friendship with a white girl. Amy Waters and I had a relationship where we didn't see color. She came from a family of evangelists who were going around the island, opening churches. Amy was the granddaughter of some of these missionaries. She was about my age at the time, maybe four or five years old. We were like a brother and sister. At that point, I didn't know the difference between Black and white. That sometimes comes later in a child's development, especially growing up in a place where Black people were the majority. I couldn't see that Amy was the whitest of white and I was among the blackest of black.

The time came when her family had to leave the island for good. We went with them to the airport. Amy and I were hugging each other really tightly and wouldn't let go of each other, because we knew she wasn't going to come back. We didn't want to lose each other. Our parents pulled us apart and took us on our way, but then we each broke loose from whoever had ahold of us, and ran back to each other, embracing and crying because we didn't want to be separated. That was my first instance of having my heart broken. We were probably too young to understand what love was, but I think that what we displayed was actually love.

In later years, this story reminded me that racism is not inherent; it's something that is taught to children. Amy and I didn't see anything wrong with the color of our skin or see how that could get in the way of our caring for each other. Now, you may say that I was too young, too innocent to know any better. But my experiences with being able to see both sides continued.

When my mother and father separated, he went to live in Aurora, Illinois, a suburb of Chicago, while she stayed in Miami. Rather than be able to see them both during the week, or one of them on the weekends, the compromise they hit on was that I would alternate entire seasons living with each of them. My seventh- and eighth-grade years I spent in Illinois. Ninth grade I did in Miami. Tenth and eleventh grades I went back and forth between Illinois and Florida, and so forth.

That may sound hard enough for an adolescent to adjust to, but it got even more interesting. When I would go live with my dad, I would attend a predominantly white school. When I would live with my mom, it was a predominantly Black school. In Florida, there were maybe three white people at our school, and the rest were Latinx, African American, or Haitian. In Illinois, there were maybe ten to fifteen African Americans and maybe five Latinxs. I was going to school in very different worlds. And I was asked to function in both of those worlds.

Those experiences of being at an all-white school alternating with being at an all-Black school taught me a lot. So many times we think we're living in completely different worlds. That might be the case when you're talking about privilege or material things. But when you're talking basic core human needs, you find all worlds are very similar. The same hierarchy you see in white schools, you see in Black schools. Who has the best clothes? Who's the fashionable girl with all the designer stuff? Who has a little more than everybody else? Who's the funny guy? Who's the smart person? Who's the nerd? People have the same fears everywhere; people have the same anxieties. The same issues that you would find among Black folks, you'd find among white folks: wanting to find love, wanting to feel like we are somebody.

By the time I graduated from high school, I could talk to anyone: Black, white, Latinx, Caribbean, and later in the army, Asian, European, you name it. All it took was being willing to really listen to someone else's perspective and being open enough to understand that another person's perspective mattered to them. And if it mattered to them, it should matter to you.

THROUGH MY WORK AT PICO, I HAD BECOME FAMILIAR WITH A NUMBER OF THE FAITH-BASED communities in Florida. These churches, synagogues, and mosques were in sync about the kind of social justice initiative we were striving to put forth on a statewide ballot, and they would end up playing a significant role in the initiative. By the time of the election, over eight hundred faith institutions supported our efforts through various means. Under the faith-specific banner of "Let My People Vote," African American, Evangelical, and Latinx Evangelical churches; synagogues; and mosques were all of one accord in support of "Second Chances." While the element of voting tends to speak to politics, what we were trying to accomplish ran much deeper than politics. This initiative was about more than that, it was about forgiveness, restoration, and love—concepts that could resonate with any major religious body as they are interwoven into the fabric of all these faiths. I felt comfortable speaking to any of those groups about what we were trying to accomplish. Because of my unique background, I was able to not only cross the color barrier but also those barriers sometimes put up between religions.

My dad, as I have said, was a preacher, and he was a serious preacher. Our family was in church a lot, Wednesday and Friday and all day Sunday for everything from services to Bible study. In my twenties, I was introduced to Islam by some very dignified and serious young men. One of the things that caught my attention when I read the Quran was that it held almost identical stories to what was in the Bible. Reading more deeply, I came to the understanding that the original book was the Torah of the Jews (the first five books of the Old Testament) and beyond that a lot of the events surrounding the major characters in all three of those books, the Old and New Testaments, and the Quran, all occurred in Egypt. The three faiths were connected as the "Abrahamic faith." So, I started reading books like the Egyptian Book of the Dead, which had symbolic links to these three major religious traditions.

All of this study helped me have a more inclusive approach to people and how they tried to solve their problems through religious practices. I came up with the analogy of a mother calling her four daughters into a kitchen and telling them, "Listen, I'm going to show you how to make my special gumbo. It's a family secret, but I want to show this recipe to you as my offspring, so when you come of age you can pass this tradition on to your families."

I could envision that mother proceeding step by step on how to make this family gumbo, and they get it. Generations down the line, those daughters have daughters, and their daughters have daughters. Now imagine at a family reunion the great-granddaughters coming together, and they're going to make great-grandma's famous gumbo. I could see those great-granddaughters in the kitchen arguing, telling each other that they're not doing it the right way, their way. Throughout the generations there have been different variations applied by different families, based on that individual's understanding and preference for what suited their needs. So, while one daughter would say, "No, the potatoes go in first," another would say, "No, no, you have to bake the potatoes, first, then you put it in there." And so forth.

Each of these great-granddaughters believe within the depths of their heart that they are the ones who have the original recipe, and the others are wrong. In a similar way, every Abrahamic religion came from the same source but took on a different personality through the generations. And now you have folks saying, "My way of thinking is the correct way, and your way is wrong. I'm the one who's going to Heaven, and you're going to Hell."

I felt that every experience I had had in my life, starting with being a Preacher's Kid, prepared me for this moment. It had set the framework for me to understand that there is more than one perspective and that I'm not always right. My view on things is not the only view and is not more legitimate than your view. We can talk it through, because we can't let different approaches and perspectives obscure the fact that we are still, at the end of the day, all just making grandma's gumbo with a twist.

SIXTEEN

# BLOOD IS THICKER THAN WATER

WHEN I FIRST STARTED becoming aware of felon disenfranchisement, it was in the context of the impact that it had on the African American and Latinx community. When you talk about felon disenfranchisement, you're talking about criminal justice. And when you're talking about criminal justice, the image that comes to your mind is an African American or maybe a Latinx person, because we've been paraded on television in that role far more frequently than anyone else. Because a lot of the attention was put on the disproportionate impact mass incarceration has had on African Americans and Latinx populations, it was natural to start thinking of felon disenfranchisement as a Black or Brown issue.

From my own previous experience, I would have been inclined to agree. In Dade County, when I looked at the people that were in the jails, there weren't a lot of white people in there. It was mostly Black and Brown people. Besides the over-policing of these communities, one of the reasons for this is the bail system. When someone is arrested, they have to post bail in order to get out. When you can't afford to do that, you have to stay in jail to fight your case from the inside. But the conditions in prison make it almost impossible to successfully fight your case while you're incarcerated. Your access to knowledge is limited. You don't have the money for investigators and can't move around to get the information you need. You're in a situation where you're basically forced to take a plea agreement. There were times when I wasn't guilty, but I took the plea because I couldn't see myself living in that jail for years at a time to make sure that my case went to trial.

When I traveled around the state talking about felon disenfranchisement, however, I met a lot of white people with felony convictions. That shifted my perspective, understanding that even though Black and Brown folks may be treated differently by the criminal justice system, that did not exclude white people from being impacted. We were the ones who were locked up, but even though they might not have been locked up, or were for far less time, they still had that felony conviction. They still couldn't vote.

Seeing the breadth of the impact let me know we had to get everybody on board if this thing was going to be successful. That was the angle that I knew we had to take in the campaign. I knew that if this issue was only seen as a Black and Brown issue, it would have not succeeded. I am unaware of any instances when this country rallied around people of color without any motive other than wanting to do the right, just, or humane thing. I had never heard or seen it before, and I didn't expect to see it now, so this had to be more than just about Black and Brown folks.

I was very intentional in going to places that were predominantly white or predominantly conservative to talk about felon disenfranchisement, because I really did believe that if I was able to break down the barriers that naturally separate us, our skin color, our political preferences, then I'd be able to connect to more people and bring more people along.

**I WAS INVITED TO SPEAK AT A COLLEGE IN SOUTHWEST FLORIDA, IN THE NAPLES AREA.** At the end of my presentation, there were a bunch of people coming up to shake my hand and take pictures. I saw this white guy standing patiently waiting to speak to me. His name was Neil Volz, and he approached me and introduced himself. He told me that he was a conservative, and he also told me that he was a returning citizen. Once I heard that, I thought, *I've got to connect with this guy. I've got to form a relationship with him.*

When we don't talk to people who we are told don't agree with us, then how do we get a chance to understand why they feel the way they feel or what they're actually thinking? Then we're judging people only by the labels we see in front of us. We don't take the opportunity to go beyond the labels and get to know the person. I wanted to know the person, whoever it was I was talking to. I wanted to know their story.

Neil's story involved coming from a small town in Ohio to becoming a high-flying lobbyist. He ended up as chief of staff for Bob Ney, one of the most powerful Republican congressmen in the nation. He got caught up in some practices that breached ethical and legal boundaries and in 2006 was convicted of conspiracy as part of the Jack Abramoff lobbying scandal. Both Neil Volz and Ney pleaded guilty to accepting lavish gifts for political favors. Ney went to prison. Volz was fined and put on probation.

When I met Neil, this guy who had been a powerful politico, he was working as a janitor because of his felony conviction. He was also working at a drug treatment shelter called Saint Matthew's House, similar, in many ways, to my experiences working at the three-quarter-way house. Right then and there, we had a common bond, not only because he was a returning citizen but also because we both worked with people who were recovering from drugs, people who had been to prison, people who had been homeless. What I know about that is when you're in proximity to those types of people, you have to have a heart. If you didn't have a heart before that, you develop one. Now, instead of looking down on people with felony convictions or with drug habits, you get to understand them more as people—another example of why breaking barriers is so important.

I wanted Neil to get involved with the Florida Rights Restoration Coalition. I felt he would bring a perspective and a voice that we needed. If we were going to really address the issues that impact people with felony convictions, we needed a cross-section of voices that have been impacted by the system, of voices that couldn't vote because of a prior felony conviction. His voice needed to be heard just like everyone else's. His perspective needed to be given consideration just like every other person's.

Neil helped create a chapter of FRRC in the area that he lived in, in southwest Florida. I got him involved in petition collection, and then, when I was putting together the advisory board and steering committee—a select group of people who would weigh in on the strategies of the campaign—it only made sense to me that Neil's voice was present in that space. He had even more relevant experience. Ironically, as a lobbyist, Neil was very influential in passing a major piece of legislation called the Help America Vote Act, getting states and localities to upgrade voting machines, registration processes, and poll-worker training after the issues of the 2000 presidential election.

Neil served as a strong voice in our campaign, especially when we were looking at how we were saying things to people, how we were engaging folks. Neil was able to find different inroads to the conservative community that we hadn't thought about. The conservative crowd had always been those other people we don't typically socialize with. When you don't interact with folks, you don't necessarily know what they do or where they do it. But Neil did. He would go to their meetings and certain events.

One time he went to a biker event and ended up meeting a guy we knew as "Rogue." Rogue was a returning citizen as well. Neil struck up a conversation with him, and they developed a relationship and, as it turned out, Rogue was the vice president of Bikers for Trump. When I heard the story, I was like, "Man, that's perfect." The power of our campaign was the fact that felon disenfranchisement impacted people from all walks of life.

For a white person to be able to look at somebody like Rogue and see that he couldn't vote because of a felony conviction totally went against their perception that disenfranchisement was a Black issue. Rogue was, to me, an amazing find, because he spoke not only to the breadth of impact that felon disenfranchisement has had but even more deeply to how we view democracy, how we view voting. It really challenged me to think through that process and realize that if we're talking about democracy and how every American citizen should have the right to vote, that means even people that I may not agree with. That means even people who may not look like me. What Rogue spoke to was the fact that we were fighting just as hard for that person who wanted to vote for Donald Trump as we were for the person who wanted to vote for Hillary Clinton. At the end of the day, if we're basing our advocacy around voting only to empower the people we believe may think like us, then we're not engaging with what democracy is all about.

I WAS NOW AWARE THAT WHEN I WENT OUT TO SPEAK ABOUT FELON DISENFRANCHISEMENT, a lot of people processed that immediately by saying: African American people are in prison. African Americans are disenfranchised. African Americans generally vote for Democrats. Through these quick, barely conscious processes that go on in people's heads, the conclusion was formed that our ballot initiative was for Democrats.

That line of thinking was based on all the misconceptions I have outlined already, but you can't grab people with that. How could I get Republicans or independents to instantly consider that we were talking about something beyond simply wanting to empower the Democratic Party, something deeper than even politics or race? So my approach to people, my initial question, was always: "Do you know someone who you love who ever made a mistake?"

Everybody knows somebody who has made a mistake, or they themselves have made a mistake. I've never had someone say no to that question. When they said yes, we would talk about it.

I would say, "You know what? That's the same thing with me. I've made a mistake. Right now, I'm here with these petitions . . ." and I'd talk about the Voting Rights Amendment. (It wasn't called Amendment 4 until later; a proposed constitutional amendment doesn't get a number until after a ballot initiative is fully approved and placed on the ballot.) I'd talk about the current policies in Florida. I'd say, "You know, in Florida, if you've ever been convicted of a felony, you lose the right to vote for life."

Almost every person I spoke to was surprised by that, that American citizens would lose their right to vote for life. People always assumed there was some kind of mechanism in place that would allow a person to gain back the right to vote once they served their time. To hear there was no such system in place in Florida and that, in fact, Florida was the worst state in the country as it relates to felon disenfranchisement, the majority of the folks I talked to expressed a range of emotions from confusion to shame.

Talking about making a mistake allowed us to start from some-place personal, not political. Even before we consulted with experts, I knew you wanted people to fight for a cause that was impacting them or people that they loved. I wanted them to see that they might have a personal stake in it. When it became about someone they loved, we were already past their partisan differences or whatever racial or other existing biases they might have. If you think about a proposed amendment as relating to faceless other people, it's easy to discard it or not put forth much effort. It's easy not to care. But when it's about you or someone you love, there's a level of care and commitment and support that significantly increases.

Once we connected our proposed amendment to someone they loved, and once we educated them about the system in place in Flor-ida, folks readily signed the petition. Blood is thicker than water. It was the same line of thinking I had been working with since I had people sign those pledge cards I printed up with PICO's help. Then I was thinking that if those 1.4 million disenfranchised returning citi-zens could each get just five of their friends and family members who loved them to pledge to vote on behalf, maybe we could convince the governor to change the clemency policies. I could imagine that each of those individuals had at least one loved one who was a registered voter and could cast a ballot.

By now we had progressed beyond trying to sway the governor, but the core logic of the effort remained: if people are going to the polls on behalf of their family members, or they're going to the polls on behalf of someone they love, chances are they're going to vote in that direction, rather than for what a policymaker is trying to con-vince them to vote for. I figured that if someone has a chance to do something on behalf of a family member, it's going to be hard to stop them from doing that. If a mother in the voting booth, for in-stance, has a moral dilemma between deciding to vote for something because of a slick-sounding politician or voting for something that will give her son or her husband a better way of life, it's not much of a dilemma in the end.

And this was what kept coming back to me about our amendment: blood is thicker than water. I can organize people along bloodlines as opposed to political lines or racial lines. We were going to win based on love and not on hate or fear. And that was going to make victory taste twice as sweet.

IMAGINE YOURSELF DRIVING DOWN THE MAJOR EXPRESSWAY IN YOUR COMMUNITY AND you come across an accident. There's someone lying on the ground and you decide to stop your car. You get out and you run up to that person.

Your first question is not going to be, "Who did you vote for, for president?" Your first question is not going to be, "How much money do you make?" Or, "What's your immigration status?" Or, "What's your sexual identity?" Your first question is going to be, "Are you okay? How can I help?"

Those moments right there are when humanity is great, when our community and our country are great. Those are moments when we can look up and be proud of who we are as Americans. Why do we have to wait for accidents to bring forth our essential humanity? Why can't we strive to act that way every moment of the day?

As the campaign wore on, I saw a spirit emerging that was similar to the spirit of communities after natural disasters.

After a hurricane goes through Florida, you see people coming together, trying to help out their neighbors. One of the images that stuck with me was from around the time Hurricane Harvey ripped through Houston. Derrick Lewis, a top-ranked UFC heavyweight who is African American, was out in his truck trying to rescue as many people as he could, as the police and firefighters were critically overloaded. One guy he was able to help had lost all of his possessions . . . except for his Confederate flag.

The flag and a few of his clothes were all he had been able to salvage. The man kept apologizing to Lewis, saying he would sit in the back of the truck and not bring the flag inside the cab, while his wife kept hitting him in the arm saying he should have just left it behind. Lewis told him, "Man, I'm not worried about that. I've been living in the South all my life, and it's nothing I haven't seen before or discussed. I just want to help."

For Lewis, like many others, the tragedy was bigger than a flag or what it represented. He was able to see beyond that symbol and beyond the skin color of that guy to see a human being in need. That is how real change happens. And that was the spirit we were embracing with the campaign. Why do we have to wait for natural disasters to show our greatness? Though our ballot initiative I thought we had the potential to elevate people over politics like that. We could come to understand how valuable and important it is for us to see each other as human beings, all just trying to overcome obstacles and deal with the challenges of life.

WHEN GOVERNOR RICK SCOTT WON HIS ELECTION IN 2010 BY JUST OVER SIXTY THOUSAND votes and was able to roll back the clemency policies that Charlie Crist had implemented, I kept thinking about the 1.4 million people in Florida who could not vote because of a felony conviction. This is not to say they would all vote in one direction, Republican or Democrat or independent or what have you. It just meant that their needs and interests were easy to overlook, because they weren't a group that politicians had to pay any attention to since they didn't have the power to vote. And even if half of returning citizens voted in a particular election, that would make a voting bloc ten times the size of the margin of victory for an election as important as one for governor of the state.

The mere sixty-thousand-vote margin in the election might have done us a favor because it energized a group of people that could actually be the catalyst to bring about change. If all it takes is sixty thousand votes to swing such an important election and the potential pool of re-enfranchised citizens is 1.4 million, that's enormous—especially in a state that has often played an outsize role in national elections. This was another major reason why restoring the power to vote felt like the first civil right to go about restoring. How powerful would it be if the very same people who were told that they don't deserve to have their voices heard could come together and create a situation in which they could be treated with dignity? Inevitably that kind of voting bloc would be able to draw attention to whatever issues it felt most strongly about.

There has been a complaint in minority communities since time immemorial that politicians don't care about the intimate issues that impact low-income families. If some members of that community have also lost their right to vote, and that is coupled with remaining folks who can vote but don't, it leads to a situation where a politician doesn't even see that community. It is very easy for a politician to ignore someone who doesn't vote. And it is a no-brainer for a politician to ignore someone who can't vote. They may not always even consciously know they're doing it, but they are just naturally drawn to pay attention to other voting blocs.

I firmly believed that a lot of our elected officials knew that the state's criminal justice policies were outdated. They knew they didn't work. But politicians don't always listen to common sense. They are scared to actually do anything to change these policies, choosing instead to feed off of a false narrative than to do the right thing, because they think it's politically safe to do so. Their decision on whether or not to revise criminal justice policies or re-entry policies is not based on data. It's not based on research. It's not based on common sense or common decency. It's based on their desire to stay in office. That is their framework of thinking.

In the case of Florida, there was a stronger force at play: private prisons. For the private prison industry, it is in their interest to create environments where more people go to prison, to fill their beds, because they are a bottom-line business and want to make profits for their stakeholders. This industry can be very influential in political campaigns. It has money and influence, and here we were battling against these people. Even if I am talking common sense as to why felon re-enfranchisement is effective, or why policies around mass incarceration are deleterious to the common good, elected officials are going to ask themselves: *Do I listen to Desmond, who is talking some common sense? Or do I listen to the donors to my campaign? I need money to get re-elected* . . . And at the end of the day, who do you think wins?

So if a lot of politicians are not guided by principles, by doing the right thing, what are they guided by? Political analysis. They are guided by their desire to remain in office. They're not hearing the cries of people in communities who are suffering. But they will listen to votes. Having a person regain that ability to vote will allow them the opportunity to have their issues paid attention to by politicians. Having an impact on elections means that politicians will pay closer attention to people's needs.

And so I thought, *Maybe we need to have a conversation with them along the lines that they understand.* Maybe I had to go over to the politicians and say, "I may not be able to influence you with money, but I can influence you with votes." And so that's what I set out to do: create a constituency group that, if we could actually organize it, would be one of the most powerful groups in the state of Florida.

# SEVENTEEN

# LET'S ROCK THIS THING

**WAS MAKING HEADWAY** with folks that I spoke with about voting along bloodlines. The average Floridian seemed to grasp what we were preaching: "Hey, this is an exciting movement that can transform the state and the country. You need to be a part of this." But up until that point, I didn't really appreciate the level of excitement there was among the grassroots folks who were helping us organize our campaign. I was holding on to faith, and that's what kept me going.

I sent an email to volunteers saying that I wanted to connect with the people in Florida who were collecting petitions. It went out maybe two days before a conference call was scheduled to take place. When that day came, I was overwhelmed because ninety-four people got on that call. Now, I didn't look at myself as anybody special. I'm not this big, bad executive director for a major organization in the state. I'm not an elected official, and yet over ninety people throughout the state of Florida got on a call to hear what I had to say.

The call lasted for probably an hour and a half. Just to hear the excitement from the folks and the different questions they were asking, to have these people affirm their belief in this issue and this movement, was a mountaintop moment for me. I thought, *With the energy of folks like this, how can we not win? How can we not be successful?* After that call, and the excitement it generated, I 100 percent believed that our initiative was going to be successful. Not without all the effort we could muster, but there was no longer any reason to be afraid.

I concluded the call by saying, "Okay, let's rock this thing."

Speaking of rocking and rolling, our cause started to be championed by some of the biggest names in show business. Whether it was supportive tweets by Rihanna or Lady Gaga or Katy Perry playing our video at one of her concerts, we had started to break in to the big time. Our biggest champion in the entertainment industry, though, was John Legend. John Legend is not just an EGOT—a winner of Emmy, Grammy, Oscar, and Tony Awards. John Legend is, and you can quote me on this, the Harry Belafonte of our time. He has been very forthright in his opposition to mass incarceration and discussing how when you lock somebody up, you are locking up their whole family with them. He gave the introduction at the Formerly Incarcerated & Convicted People and Families Movement conference in 2016, and he talked about how this issue had struck his own extended family.

At that conference, I made a connection with somebody in his camp. Word came back very quickly that he was interested in helping FRRC any way he could. He came down to Florida and performed a concert at a high school that not only supported our campaign but the organization as well. He also made a surprise visit to someone who signed a petition to support our ballot initiative. John is a beautiful spirit who believes in what's right and lends his voice to causes just like ours in a way that is amazing to watch. You just don't see that in a lot of artists.

THE REAL JOB NOW WAS TO GET AS MANY PEOPLE AS POSSIBLE TO SIGN OUR PETITION. WE had to get petitions to pass the State Supreme Court Review, and then many more after that to ensure that we could get on the ballot for 2018. The magic number we had to reach was 684,000. That is a lot of signatures to collect, but we needed even more than that, because each and every petition would go through an inspection. If individuals hadn't filled out the petition correctly, or if their street address couldn't be verified, or if it was illegible, those petitions would be declared invalid. Since some of our petitions were not going to pass the test, and since the magic number was raised to 724,000 petitions partway through our collecting them, owing to a 5 percent increase in the total number of registered Florida voters, we figured we needed to collect one million petitions. On the one hand that figure seemed astronomical; Florida only had a population of twenty-one million, to give you a sense of proportion. On the other hand, one million was a nice round, even number.

Some folks we encountered had been pretty beaten down by the political system. They felt they had been neglected so long that that neglect had turned to hopelessness. I would try to have conversations with those people one person at a time. I told people, "I understand you're angry about what's going on. You already know what you can't do. But what if we took that energy and put it toward something you can do something about?"

Part of the process was educating people, Black, white, and Brown, who were mad about the political system in this country and talking to them about how they could take their situations and turn them into power. I know that rallies and protests have their place. I just believed we had to connect with people one-on-one if we were going to convince them to use that negative energy to bring about positive results.

Typically, what happens with a ballot initiative is you get some organization or wealthy person that believes in the cause, and they'll invest first, after which you can build grassroots support for your efforts. Our ballot initiative followed the exact opposite pattern. It was led by ordinary people who were independently committed to changing the plight of disenfranchised felons; they created the tone for the campaign. Every couple of weeks we would have a call, and I would send out emails to volunteers all over the state, but the volunteers set the pace; the organizers had to try to catch up. Our volunteers were dotted all over the state, from Pensacola all the way down to Key West. They had different personalities, came from different ethnicities, and had different levels of economic status. Some were returning citizens, some were family members of returning citizens, and some just believed in the cause.

An example from the last category was Laurel Paster. Laurel was a white woman, already in her eighties when I first met her, back in 2006. She was never directly impacted by felon disenfranchisement. She'd never been to prison. But she believed in the restoration of rights. I was drawn to her from the very beginning; at every FRRC convening, she always had a smile on her face for me. I remember talking to her and finding out that she actually lived in Naples; she had driven to Orlando, which is three to four hours away, all by herself. That amazed me, that a woman of that age wanted to be a part of this convening so bad she would actually drive that long a distance.

When we started collecting petitions, she was one of the ones that kept pestering me, "I need more petitions. I need more petitions." She would collect petitions in her retirement community or go to different businesses and convince them to allow her to set up outside their store. She was that grandmother that nobody wanted to say no to. Or if you did say no to her, she'd wear you down until you said yes.

In 2011, when Governor Scott rolled back the policies of Charlie Crist and made it more difficult for returning citizens to have their rights restored, I remember calling Laurel. I've never heard her so disappointed and depressed. It was totally unlike her. She said, "I'm going to die before we ever get this thing done." That hit me hard. To think about this beautiful grandmother, who I'd come to really enjoy being around, to see her lose hope? I told her, "Don't say that!" I made a promise to her on the phone then, and I told her, "Laurel, we're going to get this thing done before you pass away. You're going to live to see us win this thing."

When we finally launched the ballot initiative, she dove in with an energy I could hardly imagine; I don't know where it came from. She was the epitome of not giving up, of believing that we can accomplish so much if we just make that effort and don't quit. At our last convening before we took the issue to the ballot, we gave her our organization's highest honor, the Presidential Award. By now she had to have somebody drive with her as she was getting weaker and weaker. From the podium she said, "Well, I thought I was retiring, but I guess Desmond is going to put me back to work. I told him I can't leave this earth until we pass this amendment."

FOLKS CAME UP WITH THEIR OWN METHODS TO COLLECT PETITIONS. EVERYBODY HAD their own unique way of doing that, but what moved me was that they came up with these ideas on their own and then went out and did it. In Pensacola, we had a woman gather a group of volunteers to collect petitions. At the time she started, we didn't have much money as an organization, so she went to an arts and crafts store and spent her own money to get a bunch of paint, then she took some regular white sheets and painted our logo on them to use as a tablecloth. In spite of our lack of resources, these volunteers were committed to finding a way to actually get this thing done.

I met one guy named Brigham, a volunteer who was passionate about the issue of felon re-enfranchisement. He was always on the calls, making suggestions, emailing me, asking what he could do to help out. Brigham made a backpack out of PVC pipes that he taped pasteboard to and wore it while he canvassed. He was now a walking advertisement for the Voting Rights Amendment with a sign that had everything spelled out, as well as a clipboard hanging from the backpack to collect signed petitions.

Brigham even made me a PVC backpack that I could wear at our 2017 convening. That summer, I wanted everybody to be a part of the gathering. This was after we had qualified to be on the ballot, and I wanted all of us to be on the same page with petition collections. Now that we were collecting petitions to make it onto the ballot for real, I wanted us to be a well-oiled machine.

I was to give the welcome speech and introduction at the beginning of the convening. I really did not know what I was going to say. The night before we were going through sound check, and our technical people asked me, "Okay, Desmond, do you want a special video? Do you want a special song? What do you want?" I was really struggling trying to figure out how I was going to open up the next morning. Then something came to me, and I said, "Find a sound piece of a heart beating." They found that, and when I got out there that next morning, everything just came to me about what I was going to say.

Four hundred people had come to our convening from all over. I got onstage and looked them in the eyes, and the heartbeat started thumping. I told the folks in that room that they were the heartbeat. All those volunteers who were going out on their own and making sacrifices of time and money—that's what this movement was all about. Folks who were directly impacted, folks with a family member who was impacted, folks who said something had to be done and in spite of this not being easy had come out and were committed every day to making sure our ballot initiative passed—they were the heartbeat. I didn't ever want to lose sight of that, because they were the lifeblood of the campaign.

**WHILE THE VOLUNTEERS WERE FANNING OUT ALL ACROSS THE STATE OF FLORIDA, I WAS** connecting with religious congregations who in the past had proven open to the concepts of redemption and social justice. The two denominations I had the most success with, as far as having access to talk to their parishioners and having the congregation be supportive in collecting petitions, were the Unitarian Universalist Association (UUA) and the African Methodist Episcopal (AME) Church.

From among so many special people in the UU community, Kindra Muntz deserves special recognition. At the time she was president of Unitarian Universalist Justice Florida, a nonprofit affiliated with the church that pursues aims related to the inherent worth and dignity of every person and to justice, equity, and compassion in human relations. It was a perfect fit for our initiative, and Kindra used her position to regularly email thousands of Unitarian Universalists directly, as well as contacting each church's administrator and Social Justice Chair individually. I knew where our completed petitions were coming from, and it always seemed to me that when I picked up a packet in the mail, it was often some Unitarian Universalist congregation that was sending it.

Bishop Adam Jefferson Richardson Jr. from the AME was another huge name that sticks out in my mind. He was in charge of the Eleventh Episcopal District, which covered the state of Florida. Coincidentally, Bishop Richardson was also involved a year before in similar efforts in Virginia. Florida was one of four states at the time, in addition to Virginia, Kentucky, and Iowa, that disenfranchised returning citizens. So Bishop Richardson knew the ropes and had a history of supporting the re-enfranchisement of people with former felony convictions.

When I was introduced to Bishop Richardson, I could tell that this issue was something he was passionate about. He was very instrumental in giving me a platform with the AME Church. When they had their convenings multiple times a year, there was always a place for me to talk to people about our efforts to collect petitions. As bishop, Richardson held a lot of sway, and he would follow me and pronounce in his stentorian voice, "And now I need you all who have heard this word to support this initiative and sign these petitions and collect as many as you can from your brothers and sisters."

Between Bishop Richardson and another pastor, Jeff Dove, who himself was a returning citizen, there was an extraordinary movement within the AME Church, with parishioners actively going out and collecting petitions and mailing packets of them to me on a weekly basis. If I ever needed anything, I could call either of those two gentlemen, and they would provide the opportunity for me to get in front of whomever I needed to get in front of.

YOU CAN IMAGINE BY NOW HOW MANY DIFFERENT CONVERSATIONS I'D HAD IN SUPPORT of the ballot initiative. As a result of all my travels, I felt that I came up with an excellent read as to what was in the hearts and minds of the average Floridian. With any campaign, you always have some polling. In the US, we poll everything. When you read a lot of these polls, you will see that they have surveyed a hundred people or a thousand people. If they got to a thousand people, it was considered a significant poll. I contrasted that to the fact that I was talking to thousands of people. I felt that gave me a particular advantage. My poll, my internal poll, was something that was up close and personal. It wasn't over the phone. It wasn't on the computer. It wasn't in a room, behind one-way mirrors. My research was me having conversations with people from all walks of life, from all political persuasions, face-to-face.

I used to bet my staff, "You give me five minutes with anyone, I don't care what their race or political preference is, I will convince them to support the Voting Rights Amendment." And I never lost that bet. I was very successful in having these conversations about second chances and forgiveness and redemption. People really got it.

I knew there was overwhelming support. In fact, throughout that process of collecting petitions, there were only two times that I actually encountered someone who I knew was definitely not going to vote for our initiative.

One was a Latinx clergyman who I ran into in a biker bar in southeast Florida. I never could figure out what a Latinx clergyman was doing in a biker bar, but there he was. No matter what I tried, no matter what I said, this guy was dead set against giving people second chances through giving them the right to vote.

The other person was a white guy who I ran into at a tailgate party for the Jacksonville Jaguars. I asked him my powerful first question, the one I always led with. This guy told me, without my bringing it up at all, "I'm voting for Trump." I said, "Okay, but do you know someone who you love that has ever made a mistake?" He said, "Yes, my son." Internally, I thought, *Yup, I got him! I got him. I'm going to convince him based on love.*

I said, "After he's served his time, don't you want your son to be able to vote?"

This guy looked me straight in the eyes and said, "Hell, no! He's too damn stupid. I don't ever want him to vote."

When he told me that, I knew that was it. I'm not going to proceed further with this guy. If you don't even want your own son to vote, then you're not going to have empathy for a bunch of people you don't know. So I moved on. Those were the only two times that I can specifically remember when I walked away knowing that that person is not going to vote for our initiative. For everyone else, I could feel a connection when we talked. For most of us have someone, a friend or a family member, who deserves a second chance, and even if they don't, most people just believe in fundamental fairness or forgiveness.

# EIGHTEEN

# THE HOME STRETCH

**W**HEN I WAS IN RECOVERY, my prayers were always about wanting to do God's will. They started out simply. On any given day, my mission was to not use drugs and to do something that would make somebody's life better, even if it was just to make them smile. I wanted to learn something new and to be a better person than I was the day before, understanding that I'm not going to be perfect and it's not about the end. It's not about reaching your final destination. It's about the journey.

I tried with all my might to hang on to that message as we got closer and closer to having our ballot initiative become the focus of national and even international attention. The journey is where everything fits. I kept that in the back of my mind, not to pray for personal gain but for the wisdom and the strength to be the best that I could be. If winning a fight is what would bring that about, then let's win. If losing a fight is what would bring that about, then who am I to object?

WE WERE COLLECTING OUR PETITIONS UP AND DOWN THE STATE OF FLORIDA AT A STEADY clip. But I didn't realize what kind of paradigm shift in our exposure was possible until comedian Samantha Bee of the TBS show *Full Frontal* featured our ballot initiative. That was a game changer and put us out there like nothing had before. Before showing the six-minute clip that featured me and Neil Volz, we had about seventy thousand petitions signed. After that episode aired, we were swamped with people mailing in petitions. In spite of the hundreds of thousands of miles I'd driven around Florida, and all the conversations I had, the people who I talked to represented a drop in the bucket. At the time, we didn't have money for advertising. The campaign was moved through word of mouth; that was how we were able to build momentum and raise awareness. Being on national television allowed us to reach all kinds of living rooms we wouldn't have had access to, either because we didn't have the connections or because there are only so many hours in the day. Now it seemed I couldn't go a whole day without someone stopping to tell me, "Hey, we saw you on Samantha Bee!"

Initially, a young man named Tyler, who was working for *Full Frontal*, reached out to us. What I have come to understand is that even for a national show, there is more often than not a local connection, somebody on the team who either lives in Florida or used to live in Florida. That was the case with Tyler, who told me, "We're interested in doing something around your efforts." We were game for it. Every little bit helped.

They filmed two segments. For the first one, they came down to Florida and filmed us in West Palm Beach. I spoke at an event there, and they had a table where we were getting people to sign petitions. The camera crew followed us to the hotel and filmed us talking to people and collecting more petitions. The second segment we filmed in the studio in New York, where we spoke with Samantha. Our conversation flowed so naturally. Nothing was scripted, and it came out amazing.

We were so appreciative of Samantha Bee, because there are plenty of folks who will air an episode about something and that's that. But the folks at *Full Frontal* actually created a website for us and encouraged people to fill out the petition, which you could download at home. That, to me, went above and beyond. This was not just a show to highlight an issue. Samantha Bee changed the game.

A few months after that, John Oliver did a piece on us that actually helped to bolster the work started by *Full Frontal*. I even went on Fox to talk to Tucker Carlson about felon re-enfranchisement. It didn't matter if the show was conservative or progressive; I wanted to spread the message to everybody.

Carlson was advancing his own agenda, but he wasn't totally against us. And his own viewers were siding with us. We heard people saying that yes, they were conservative, but this was the right thing to do or that we were onto something here. There were folks who were Republican but were impacted by being disenfranchised and were speaking out.

That was very encouraging to me and got to the root of what I had been saying all along. Too often we limit ourselves on certain campaigns or movements, because we assume there are certain audiences we can't be in front of. We limit who we talk to, but when we limit who we talk to, we limit the number of people to support us. Then we allow other folks to form their own opinions without even having a conversation about it. I was always of the mindset that said, "No, this is an all-American issue. We need to get buy-in from everyone." Just like when I first started collecting petitions, I went straight to conservative people. Others might say, "Oh no, conservative people are going to be against your initiative because they think this only helps Democrats." To which I replied, "No, this is for everybody. People who vote Democrat are not the only people who get in trouble." No matter what your political party is, you can lose your right to vote.

Being bold and not setting up walls and being willing to go in front of any audience to talk about this was all made easier because, at the end of the day, I knew that what I was talking about was honorable. What I was talking about was based on values that are shared by everyone, especially when you talk about forgiveness and redemption and restoration. I looked forward to being in front of audiences others might be convinced would not agree with me. I have been successful with that more often than not.

WHEN I LOOKED AT ALL THE MAIL THAT WAS COMING IN NOW BECAUSE OF OUR NATIONAL exposure, I felt buoyed about our chances of success. If you think about it, someone had to actually go to a site to see the petition. They had to download it, then print it out. They had to sign the petition. Then they had to put it in an envelope, address the envelope, put a stamp on it, and mail it. That's a lot of steps someone is taking to support this. I could not help but believe that if someone would take the time to go through all that to give us a petition, then getting them to eventually vote for our cause was not going to be as big of a deal.

I had people actually write me letters, using their own stamps to connect with our cause. I had never experienced that before. Donations were coming in from major and minor sources alike, and from people as far away as Washington State and Massachusetts—you couldn't get much farther away from Florida than that.

Some folks were contributing recurring donations; every month that twenty dollars would come from someone out of Seattle or that fifty dollars from someone in San Francisco. We were able to start hiring staff, and we got an office. We had a campaign manager. All of that was great. Throughout this process, though, even as we were getting professionalized, the one thing I was very adamant about was that we could not fail to recognize the heartbeat. We could not lose sight of the people who were directly impacted. We could not lose sight of all of the volunteers and that grassroots spirit that kept the campaign afloat. We couldn't lose that identity.

Once we had collected enough petitions, or more than enough petitions, we braced ourselves for what was purported to be the next battle. We were told that a tough fight awaited us in the Florida State Supreme Court before we could get on the ballot for 2018. Either the state attorney general was going to oppose it or groups on the outside would submit an amicus brief saying that our initiative should not be allowed to move forward. There was also a fiscal impact conference. At the same time the State Supreme Court does its review, the State of Florida holds hearings and invites people to discuss the economic impact of a particular amendment on the state. For instance, if a certain amendment passes, is it going to cost Florida's taxpayers a certain amount of money? If not, is it going to save the taxpayers money? Those fiscal impact statements are always attached to any amendment that makes the ballot.

None of these bad things actually happened. The state attorney general didn't challenge the validity of the ballot; she conceded to its constitutionality. No one submitted an amicus brief against our amendment. If there was an amicus brief, it was one that was submitted for our amendment, not against. The State Supreme Court approved our language (constitutional language)! Now we had to collect enough signatures to get it on the ballot! The language says:

> No. 4 Constitutional Amendment Article VI, Section 4. *Voting Restoration Amendment.* This amendment restores the voting rights of Floridians with felony convictions after they complete all terms of their sentence including parole or probation. The amendment would not apply to those convicted of murder or sexual offenses, who would continue to be permanently barred from voting unless the Governor and Cabinet vote to restore their voting rights on a case by case basis.

The Florida Division of Elections approved the language on April 20, 2018, for the election that coming November. We were to be Amendment 4.

Between April 20 and November 6, Election Day, our efforts were all-consuming. There was no more back burner. We had passed a certain threshold. It needed to be all systems go. If something cropped up on my path that wouldn't actually benefit the ballot initiative, I would not spend much time on it. This was something serious, and I had to remain keenly focused on the work we were doing. The vote itself might be months away, but there was no time to waste. I'd always heard that when you do ballot initiatives, you only get one bite at the apple. I had to make sure that bite counted.

We had to make sure that our issue did not fade from people's minds, but we wanted to stay true to the core of the message at the same time. We still wanted to connect felon re-enfranchisement in the mind of voters to someone they knew and someone they loved. I continued to travel around the state, visiting colleges and talking to kids about Amendment 4; some of their parents were impacted by felon disenfranchisement. I went on radio shows, such as *Hot Talk*, hosted by Jill Tracey, which reached the Miami area, and Monica May in Orlando, who hosted *The Tom Joyner Morning Show*. I would be on the radio in northwest Florida. I would be on the radio in South Florida. I would talk to anyone and everybody about this.

In Florida, the primaries are held in August; the ballot initiatives aren't on the primary ballots, of course, but it was a chance to talk to voters. By now we were very familiar with the voting locations and aware of the opportunity that presented itself to us there. In August of 2018, we fanned out across all of the polling places, passing out materials and reminding people to vote "Yes on 4" in November.

This period could best be summed up by the convening we had before the election. I came out to give the introductory speech, but this time the soundtrack wasn't a heartbeat. This time it was the opening of the song "Lose Yourself" by Eminem, where he asks if you had only one shot at everything you ever wanted, would you really let it slip? The message was, This is our moment. No one ever thought we'd get this far without major funding. No one ever thought this controversial issue would make the ballot. But here we are, and we have a choice. Are we going to seize this moment and give it all we got?

Publicly I had to put on my best face, while privately the campaign was wearing on me. Our polling numbers were high; that wasn't the problem. We were polling consistently well throughout the entire state, which was an amazing feat in and of itself, because in Florida, what the polls say in south Florida isn't necessarily what the polls say in north Florida. To be polling well in every area of Florida brought a level of confidence.

My concerns came from the unexpected. I didn't know if some misleading attack ads were going to drop at any minute, from a previously unknown group, and if they did, what kind of impact that would have. I also bore a pressure that I never revealed to anyone, but it was a weight that I carried on my shoulders for so long. Typically, when you see a campaign like ours, the person at the helm of those campaigns is not somebody who's Black. It's going to be somebody white, with an impressive resume, somebody who's well-connected. Here I was, a Black person. Not only a Black person, but a formerly incarcerated person who was leading this.

There is an implicit bias that in order for something to be successful, somebody white has to be leading it. The reality is that there are so many talented African American and Latinx Americans, so many people of color, who have the capacity to actually lead things. Typically what you see is those people as a deputy or second in command. But the ultimate person calling the shots does not look like me and definitely does not have the background that I had. I didn't want our initiative losing to be an excuse for people not to trust the leadership

of returning citizens. I didn't want our losing to be an excuse for people not to trust the leadership of a Black person. They might not say
it out loud, but that would be the implicit understanding for many
people as to why people of color are not at the helm of major movements and major campaigns.

That was something that stayed with me. And then there was just
the relentlessness of the timeline for the initiative. When you think
about a campaign, most last a year or less. I was like that person who
was running for office, but I had been on the campaign trail for over
four years. That's every day, waking up, thinking about the issue of
felon disenfranchisement and problems associated with the issue and
connecting the dots, thinking about the campaign and doing something to further it. It was a constant grind, twenty-four hours a day,
seven days a week. I hadn't taken a real vacation where I was able to
totally unplug in years.

While there were other organizations that strongly supported
Amendment 4 and were engaged in the campaign, none of them had
committed 100 percent. They had their own organizational missions
that led them to other issues they had to deal with. Amendment 4 was
all there was for FRRC. We put everything on the line for it. We put
everything on the table.

I had been struggling with diverticulitis for a while. Then the stress
of a multiyear campaign, constant worrying and being on the go,
not eating right or sleeping enough, day after day, caused me to have
flare-ups. I didn't realize the toll that it was taking on me. There were
a couple of times when I came very close to having a rupture that
could've been devastating to me. Doctors kept telling me I needed surgery, but I was scared that if I took any time off, the movement would
stop. When my condition finally became too severe, I had no choice
but to go under the knife. I finally had surgery in 2018, during the campaign. They had to cut out parts of my intestines. When I looked at the
wounds on my stomach, I thought, *This campaign literally took a chunk
of me. This is my pound of flesh I had to sacrifice for the cause.*

Those last months had been really, really rough. But now they
were over. All of the time I had spent wondering if Amendment 4
was going to pass or not, if we were going to go down in flames or we
were going to be victorious, came down to one night. We had a watch

party at a house we rented just for this purpose, and it was starting to fill with people who were waiting on me. I did not want to know the results. I was made aware of all the media coverage we were getting; we were in the middle of the spotlight of the country—in some cases, the world, because news outlets globally were covering tonight's results. I was hiding away, because I knew I was going to have to do one of two things: I was going to have to give a victory speech, or I was going to have to somehow or other give a speech that would continue to inspire people in spite of the fact that we had lost.

As I mentioned, I rarely write any notes before I speak, preferring just to let what I have to say come from my heart and matching that to the temperature in the room. My wife came to check on me a few times while we were waiting for the election results, but basically everyone else just left me alone. Then I got the call to come down to the ballroom; it was getting close to that time. As soon as I walked in the door, that's when it was announced that we had won. I saw so many elated faces. I didn't have a clue who had been invited to the watch party; I was not involved in the planning of it. So many folks were hugging me as I tried to make my way to the stage. We got over 350,000 more votes than we needed to pass the initiative; we needed 60 percent of the vote total, and we got almost 65 percent. Over five million people had voted "Yes on 4."

When we won Amendment 4, I knew how important it was. But even I didn't grasp just how important. Every time someone would talk to me about what had just been accomplished, it would start to overwhelm me, and I would just shut down because the thought of the magnitude of what we did was too much for my mind to bear.

The minute we won, and for days and weeks and months afterward, my cell phone and my office phone were bombarded. I was receiving emails and instant messages from folks who were returning citizens, who were besides themselves with excitement, wanting to know where they could register to vote.

I also got hounded by people who wanted to know where the list of returning citizens was so they could register them right away. When folks called me to ask that questions, I would say: "Where do you think they are? Do you think there's a special place that people with felony convictions hang out? No, they're in our homes, in our communities, at the shopping centers, churches. There's no special place for returning citizens." I started feeling like returning citizens were going to be turned into some pawn in a partisan battle, that folks were just wanting to seek out people like me and register me because they thought I must be a Democrat and that they'd never have to worry about losing a race again.

That showed me how we reduce people's humanity, and that went against what Amendment 4 was all about. We were about lifting up a person's humanity and connecting with each other along those lines. To now be experiencing this onslaught of requests for returning citizens, it opened my eyes to one of the reasons why I think a lot of Americans who are registered don't even bother to go vote. Are we being seen as individuals with specific concerns on our minds and in our communities? Or are we just looked at as more votes to add to the coffers? Should registering people to vote be a purely transactional interaction, or should it be more of a transformational one? The driving force behind registering people to vote should be the belief that the more people participate in elections, the more accountable politicians will be to the voters, and the more vibrant our democracy will become.

After I registered for the first time, I went on the news station in Orlando, and a reporter popped the question. I knew it was going to come at some point. "Did you register as a Democrat or a Republican?"

My answer was, "I registered with no party affiliation."

The reason why I did that is because I believe that I fought too hard and waited too long to get my voting rights back to give it away to just anybody. I really felt that as returning citizens, we have an opportunity to shake up the status quo. When you looked at the state of politics today, there is such a hard partisan divide. What you see is partisan bickering, not coming together and trying to forge some type of compromise. You see a lot of the civility erode in our political system, where folks are hurling insults at each other and refusing to sit down and have conversations to find their common ground, to see where the connections are or where there's alignment or agreement.

I may have shocked a lot of people when I registered with no party affiliation (NPA), but returning citizens are such a large force in

Florida. We now potentially have a new voting constituency of over a million people. If we allow ourselves to be consumed by the Democrats and the Republicans, it will continue to be business as usual. We actually have an opportunity to shake up the status quo and force both sides to really rethink how they are going about their business. That was my thinking.

Let's restore the joy of voting instead. Amendment 4 could be more than just about returning citizens being able to register to vote. It could be about more than even a celebration of an expansion of democracy. It could shift the entire culture around voting. And what better person is there to talk to people about how valuable the right to vote is, and how we honor that by actually voting, than someone who has lost the right to vote and has had to fight to get it back? We could engage in conversations with everyone and create a movement that will re-energize folks. There are so many people in our country who are registered to vote but don't vote. There are so many people who are eligible to register to vote but don't want to be registered. We could create an environment that makes voting exciting again, something that people look forward to doing rather than feeling it's something they have to do, like it is some burden they have to bear. We can take this moment and parlay it into a much bigger moment of engaging American citizens throughout the country, letting that energy and excitement be contagious. That is why Amendment 4 passed, because it brought people together across political and racial lines to agree on something and to move something forward out of love.

# LOVE WILL WIN THE DAY

A MENDMENT 4 ACCOMPLISHED what it was intended to do. Some may disagree with this statement in light of the legislative and litigative battles that ensued immediately after our ballot initiative passed, and the dominance of the narrative that created the need to "fight to save" the amendment from the malicious intent of conservative legislators. The reality was that in spite of the legislation that emerged and was eventually challenged in court, the accomplishment of Amendment 4 remained intact. Prior to the passage of Amendment 4, anyone convicted of any felony offense lost their civil rights, including the right to vote, for life. The seriousness or the triviality of the offense did not matter. Upon conviction, the only chance a person had to regain the right to vote was through clemency, which meant that one had to avail oneself of the mercy of the governor, a politician. It didn't matter how deserving one might be. It didn't matter if there was a victim or not, or if there was a victim; it didn't matter if that victim was in favor of clemency. The decision to grant clemency was arbitrary and seemed to boil down to how the governor felt at the time and his partisan leanings. As arduous and arbitrary the process was, though, it was the only option returning citizens had if they ever wanted to vote in Florida. That is, until Amendment 4 passed.

Amendment 4 enshrined the right to vote in the Florida constitution, unless that right was removed or amended by the same process that FRRC had led, with the help of so many Florida voters. Through the efforts of everyone connected with Amendment 4, we had more than a flag-waving patriotic moment on January 8, 2019. We had a watershed moment in history, when people became full citizens again. Unfortunately, partisan rancor raised its head again, and the very next day we got a call from the leadership in Tallahassee saying that they wanted to talk to us about where all this was going. I didn't think there was anything to talk about; the highest authority in the land, the state constitution, clearly stated how we were moving forward. No state officeholder, no supervisor of elections, could supersede that.

And, yet, the politicians still wanted to engage in conversations about the restitution aspect of "completion of sentence." Recall that the ballot initiative amendment restored the voting rights of Floridians with felony convictions after they completed *all terms* of their sentence, including parole or probation. Whatever these terms involved from a financial perspective was now at issue.

We often hear politicians bemoan judges who "legislate from the bench," yet somehow we now saw some of those same leaders suggesting that it was the proper role of the legislature, and not the judiciary, to "interpret the constitution." The reason Floridians from all walks of life worked together to collect more than one million signatures to get Amendment 4 on the ballot was because partisanship prevented our state lawmakers from doing what was right. Rather than allowing the process to work itself out, members of the state legislature now took it upon themselves to decide what that process should be.

Central to the legislative process was the question of what constituted "completion of sentence." The decision to address this question opened up a Pandora's box from which emerged claims of racism, allegations of "poll taxes," debates that revealed again the sharp partisan divide that Amendment 4 seemed to have started to mend, as well as an impending lawsuit that would capture the attention of the country.

In a sense, I suspected that something like this was going to happen. I know that we don't live in a perfect world and that the "ideal" situation doesn't always play out the way it should, but I had hope. Didn't we just pass Amendment 4 the ideal way? So you can't really blame me for thinking that maybe, just maybe, politicians would keep their hands off of this beautiful victory and allow Amendment 4 to run its course unencumbered. I guess they couldn't help themselves.

The way I looked at what the legislature was doing was like this: For years, Florida politicians walked by a homeless family and never lifted a finger to help them. One day, citizens decided that enough was enough, so they took matters into their own hands because they believed that people should be treated better. These citizens came together and built the homeless family a house, but as soon as the house was completed, those same politicians barged into the new home and demanded that they, the politicians, should be able to decide how the home would be decorated.

When there is alignment between the State Senate, House, and governor, and they are all dominated by one party; whatever they want to happen will happen. We were thus left with no choice but to roll up our sleeves and try to mitigate any potential damage. Central to our efforts were the roughly 1.4 million Floridians who were just given the opportunity to be a part of our democracy again. These were real people with real lives, not just statistics, or votes for any particular party. We were more influenced by the desire to expand democracy to everyone and by the desire to restore a voice to countless Americans with felony convictions. In a perfect world, people, not politics, would be central to the debate, but like I've said, we don't live in a perfect world.

So the debates began, and as predicted, they fell along partisan lines with conservative lawmakers leaning on comments made during oral arguments in the Florida Supreme Court review of our ballot language. In an argument to the State Supreme Court, our attorney had made comments, in a different context, about fines, fees, and financial obligations being included in a sentence. The purpose of that hearing was to assess whether Amendment 4's language comported with the constitutional requirements for a citizens' ballot initiative. The question came out of nowhere, our attorney answered it on the fly, and we were forced to live with that answer; an answer that became the foundation of what the leadership in Tallahassee decided to work from.

After weeks of debate and over our strenuous objection, the Florida legislature passed a measure requiring people with felony records to pay all financial obligations ("court fees, fines, and restitution") from their sentencing except in two cases. The first is that a judge, with the consent of the victim of a crime in such cases where that applies, can dismiss the repayment requirement. The second allows a judge to convert all fines, fees, and restitution into community-service hours. In the second case, a person could have their voting rights restored after completing community service.

We argued that since tracking fines, fees, and restitution is so complicated in Florida, with no single entity holding all the information, people wouldn't even know the amount they owed. We also argued that the courts were going to be bent to the point of breaking with an influx of people seeking to have their financial obligations dismissed or converted to community service.

Central to the fines and fees argument was the question of how many of the 1.4 million returning citizens would be impacted by this new spin. How many will be able to immediately register to vote, and how many would have to pay off their legal financial obligations before being eligible to vote? That was a simple question that did not have a simple answer. One estimate indicated that approximately 840,000 out of the 1.4 million returning citizens would be eligible to vote immediately. Another estimate indicated the inverse: that over 800,000 returning citizens still had some type of financial obligation that would prevent them from registering to vote. This variation between the two estimates hinged on what was being included in the assessment of what constituted legal financial obligations. In the first case, only fines, fees, and restitution were considered in the assessment. That was in line with what were thought to be the only financial obligations that could be attached to the actual crime a person was convicted of committing. The other assessment included court costs. While both assessments fell short of the 1.4 million returning citizens we would have ideally wanted to be able to vote immediately, I was still optimistic, because the 2018 elections showed me that Florida's governor's race was decided by thirty thousand votes, a congressional race was decided by sixteen thousand votes, and generally presidential elections in Florida are decided by approximately one hundred thousand votes. Out of either estimate of how many returning citizens would have to satisfy their legal financial obligations, there still remained an estimated six hundred thousand to eight hundred thousand returning citizens in Florida who would be able to register immediately. That number "covers the gap" for any election in Florida and means that even though the debate and the litigation may rage on, the voices of people impacted by the criminal justice system can still be heard at the ballot box, and their voices can be loud enough to determine who our next governor, member of Congress, or even president of the United States will be. In spite of the barriers raised by meeting legal financial obligations, there are still enough returning citizens who can play a critical role in local elections to determine the next state attorney or district attorney, sheriff, judge, public defender, clerk of court, or even supervisor of elections in their counties. I'm optimistic because people who've long been impacted by our broken criminal justice system, and who have long been silenced, now have an opportunity to play a significant role in fixing it.

As anticipated, a lawsuit quickly followed, challenging the Amendment 4 legislation. Filed in a federal court in the Northern District of Florida, sixteen plaintiffs asked the court to determine whether or not it is constitutional to deny a person the right to vote solely because the person is financially incapable of paying legal financial obligations in a felony case that is essentially closed. The court initially issued a ruling on a motion for a preliminary injunction and held that the plaintiffs could not be denied the right to vote if they could not afford to pay their financial obligations. The state lost its appeal of that decision, and the actual trial is slated to begin in 2020. Of note is the fact that the lawsuit is now a class-action suit. While the previous court ruling technically only applied to the sixteen named plaintiffs, this "class-action" designation means that subsequent rulings from the court would now apply more broadly to the 1.4 million returning citizens.

As of this writing there is still uncertainty about the final outcome of the lawsuit. The case could potentially go all the way to the US Supreme Court, but in spite of the uncertainty, the Amendment 4 victory has created a moment for returning citizens like me, a moment that has reignited a dormant hope, stimulated the imagination of a more inclusive and vibrant democracy, and repositioned the balance of electoral power. This moment has given me and many others in Florida and throughout the country the chance to firmly declare "Our Vote, Our Voice, Our Time!"

And no matter the challenges that may lay ahead, I still believe that love will win the day.

# ACKNOWLEDGMENTS

ONE NIGHT WHILE I was in drug treatment, I got on my knees to pray. This was probably *the* moment when I had finally come to terms with who I was that led me to drug treatment, who I was at that very moment when I was on my knees, and the uncertainty of who I would become from that night forth. I remember telling God that night what would from that moment on become the foundation to all of my prayers even today. I asked God to give me the strength, stamina, and discernment to be able to do his will, and even though I had no clue as to where my dedication would eventually lead me, I promised God that wherever he took me, I would always let folks know who got me there. So, first and foremost, I give thanks to my higher power, whom I choose to call God, for choosing and allowing me to do his work, and for the fires he took me through to prepare me.

This book is also dedicated to the over six million people in the United States who are incarcerated, the countless millions with previous felony convictions, and the families who have a loved one who has been impacted by an imperfect criminal justice system. I pray that this book will serve as a testament to the power of hope, redemption, and love; that any past mistakes do not have to become a continuous indicator of who we are but rather one of many ingredients that shape who we are today and enhance who we become.

I want to thank the countless philanthropists whose generosity, commitment to justice, and financial and moral support contributed to the successful passing of Amendment 4.

To Eric Brakken, who tore up many of my first proposals for a ballot initiative (I know he'll dispute this account) and helped me set the framework for a "pathway to victory." To Muhammad Malik and Jose Luis Marantes, who would spend countless hours talking about "the Movement" and dreaming big. To Norris Henderson of VOTE NOLA, which provided an example of the potential power that people with felony convictions possess—thank you.

I would also like to thank Susan and Regan Pritzker, whose support and belief in me made this book possible; Antonio Cediel, who was the motivating force that made me stop only "thinking" about writing a book and actually start writing; Stuart Horwitz, who provided detailed and speedy editorial support; and Helene Atwan of Beacon Press, who believed in this book and my vision from the beginning.

My biggest thank-yous are, of course, reserved for my family.

To my many brothers, sisters, nieces, and nephews, who saw my journey firsthand and never wavered in their love for me; to my brother Jerry, whose untimely death drove home the connectivity we all share as human beings. And to my extended family: though we were not connected by blood, our bond was just as strong if not stronger. I love you all.

When I first met my wife, Sheena, I recognized that she was God's gift to me. It wasn't what I wanted; it was what I needed. Everybody wants that companion. We go out looking for that person who's going to be our life partner, and I recognize that. We have five kids, and I love each and every last one of them. They were not kids from our marriage, but that doesn't matter; I don't call them my stepkids. They're my kids. I embrace them, and they have fully embraced me.

My kids did not take to the campaign easily, and I couldn't blame them. They were seven to seventeen years old between them, and they were into things that any normal kid would be into. Their world consisted of TV, video games, playing sports, and exploring the woods in our backyard, so when I had them counting petitions in batches of fifty in preparation of sending them out to volunteers, it seemed as if I was asking them to do some insurmountable chore. If I was any of their ages, I would have felt the same way, but what other choice did I have? It had to get done, and I already had too much on my plate, so grudgingly they counted. It wasn't until the last leg of the campaign, when they would accompany me at an event or a bus-tour stop, that I believe that the significance of what I was doing and the importance of the role they played started to sink in. When they started seeing so many people approaching me to talk about how felon disenfranchisement had impacted their lives or the life of a loved one, or when they started seeing the reaction of the crowd when I was speaking, they started to get a sense that what we were working on, what they were forced to work on, was part of a movement that was poised to not only transform the state of Florida but also the country and the world. When they finally started to see the bigger picture, I didn't have to force them to engage anymore. They took pride in whatever they did. They bought into the campaign, and even if they didn't immediately say it, they were proud to be a part of it, and they were proud of their father.

Their admiration for me and my work served as a bit of a reprieve for the guilt I was carrying around. The campaign had demanded basically all of my time. It had consumed me so much that I felt that I had failed my kids. I missed parent-teacher conferences. I missed a lot of football practices and games. When they played Pop Warner football on Saturdays, I was usually traveling somewhere in the state, picking up petitions, delivering petitions, or speaking at some event that I felt I could not afford to miss. As a former football player, I had the same dream of many fathers who played the sport. I yearned to be able to teach them some of the things I had learned while playing football. I yearned to attend their practices and yell at their coach if I felt the coach messed up, or even become an assistant coach. I wanted to be there for every moment of their athletic lives, but the campaign wouldn't allow it. I was forced to live with the fact that I missed many moments in their young adolescent lives, moments that I would never get back. What I know now is that the harsh reality is that if you are committed to a movement or a cause, there are going to be some painful sacrifices that you are going to have to make. There is no triumph without sacrifice. There is no movement without pain.

Today I look back at my family and beam with pride. My oldest son, Xavier, is our audiovisual specialist and works in the communications department of FRRC. He has managed to evolve into a producer of award-worthy videos. My second-oldest son, Xandre, the one who gave me the hardest time about counting petitions, became one of our most dependable volunteers, led our texting campaign, which contacted over one million voters to support Amendment 4, and is now my executive assistant. My third-oldest son, Nathan, who just graduated from high school, volunteers to assist the with logistics and helps out around the office from time to time. Our youngest two children are still in school. My daughter Xcellence helped to run our "souls to the polls" effort in Orlando and is still a constant administrative volunteer and an active leader of Black Youth Vote. Our youngest, Xzion, was the first to understand the significance of our campaign, probably because he was the first of my kids to accompany me to collect petitions. Combined, my family sits with God at the center of my universe, and I pray that they will all be pleased with this work.

# ABOUT THE AUTHOR

**DESMOND MEADE** is the president of the FRRC (Florida Rights Restoration Coalition), chair of Floridians for a Fair Democracy, and a graduate of Florida International University College of Law. As a formerly homeless returning citizen, he fought to restore voting rights to approximately 1.4 million Floridians with past felony convictions. He was recognized by *Time* as one of the 100 Most Influential People in the World in 2019. Today, Desmond continues fighting against new restrictions placed on Florida voters that have been likened to Jim Crow laws. Desmond and his wife and five children live in Florida.

**THE FLORIDA RIGHTS RESTORATION COALITION** is a grassroots membership organization run by returning citizens (formerly convicted persons) who are dedicated to ending the disenfranchisement and discrimination against people with convictions and to creating a more comprehensive and humane reentry system to enhance successful reentry, reduce recidivism, and increase public safety.